S0-ACG-981

THE REVELS PLAYS

General Editor: Clifford Leech

THE ATHEIST'S TRAGEDY,
OR, THE HONEST MAN'S REVENGE

THE
ATHEIST'S
TRAGEDIE:
OR
The honeſt Man's Reuenge.

As in diuers places it hath often beene Acted.

WRITTEN
By *Cyril Tourneur.*

AT LONDON,
Printed for *Iohn Stepneth,* and *Richard Redmer,* and are to
be ſold at their Shops at the Weſt end of Paules.
1611.

The Atheist's Tragedy,

or,

The Honest Man's Revenge

CYRIL TOURNEUR

EDITED BY
IRVING RIBNER

THE REVELS PLAYS

METHUEN & CO LTD
LONDON

This edition first published 1964

FOR
DICK TAYLOR
(1910–1962)

General Editor's Preface

The Revels Plays began to appear in 1958, and in the General Editor's Preface included in the first few volumes the plan of the series was briefly sketched. All those concerned in the undertaking recognized that no rigid pattern could be proposed in advance: to some extent the collective experience of the editors would affect the series as it developed, and the textual situation was by no means uniform among the plays that we hoped to include. The need for flexibility is still recognized, and each editor indicates in his introduction the procedures that have seemed best in relation to his particular play.

Nevertheless, we were fairly convinced that in some matters our policy would remain constant, and no major change in any of these respects has been made. The introduction to each volume includes a discussion of the provenance of the text, the play's stage-history and reputation, its significance as a contribution to dramatic literature, and its place within the work of its author. The text is based on a fresh examination of the early editions. Modern spelling is used, archaic forms being preserved only when rhyme or metre demands them or when a modernized form would not give the required sense or would obscure a play upon words. The procedure adopted in punctuation varies to some extent according to the degree of authority which an editor can attribute to the punctuation of the copy-text, but in every instance it is intended that the punctuation used in a Revels volume should not obscure a dramatic or rhetorical suggestiveness which may be discerned in the copy. Editorial stage-directions are enclosed in square brackets. The collation aims at making clear the grounds for an editor's choice wherever the original or a frequently accepted modern reading has been departed from. Annotations attempt to explain difficult passages and to provide such comments and illustrations of usage as the editor considers desirable.

When the series was planned, it was intended that each volume should include a glossary. At an early stage, however, it was realized that this would mean either an arbitrary distribution of material between the glossary and the annotations or a duplication of material. It has therefore become our practice to dispense with a glossary but to include an index to the annotations, which avoids duplication and facilitates reference.

Act-divisions are employed if they appear in the copy-text or if the structure of the play clearly points to a five-act division. In other instances, only scene-numbers are inserted. All act- and scene-indications which do not derive from the copy-text are given unobtrusively in square brackets. In no instance is an editorial indication of locality introduced into a scene-heading. When an editor finds it necessary to comment on the location of a scene, this is done in the annotations.

The series continues to use the innovation in line-numbering that was introduced in the first volume. Stage-directions which occur on lines separate from the text are given the number of the immediately preceding line followed by a decimal point and 1, 2, 3, etc. Thus 163.5 indicates the fifth line of a stage-direction following line 163 of the scene. At the beginning of a scene the lines of a stage-direction are numbered 0.1, 0.2, etc.

The Revels Plays have begun with the re-editing of a number of the best-known tragedies and comedies of the later Elizabethan and Jacobean years, and there are many such plays to which the techniques of modern editing need to be applied. It is hoped, however, that the series will be able to include certain lesser-known plays which remain in general neglect despite the lively interest that an acquaintance with them can arouse.

It has always been in the forefront of attention that the plays included should be such as deserve and indeed demand performance. The editors have therefore given a record (necessarily incomplete) of modern productions; in the annotations there is, moreover, occasional conjecture on the way in which a scene or a piece of stage-business was done on the original stage. Perhaps, too, the absence of indications of locality and of editorial scene-headings will suggest the advantage of achieving in a modern theatre some approach to the characteristic fluidity of scene and the neutrality of acting-space that Shakespeare's fellows knew.

CLIFFORD LEECH

Toronto, 1963

Contents

Frontispiece: The title page of the 1611 Quarto. Reproduced
by courtesy of the Trustees of the British Museum.

Preface

In preparing this edition of *The Atheist's Tragedy* I have been very
fortunate in having Professor Allardyce Nicoll's work on the play
to guide me and in the assistance which has come to me from so
many quarters. From the American Council of Learned Societies
and the Huntington Library have come grants-in-aid for which I
am very grateful; to Dr John E. Pomfret and his staff at the Huntington, Miss Mary Isabel Fry in particular, I am indebted for every
kind of assistance and for the opportunity to work for two summers
in the most beautiful and congenial of surroundings. At the Folger
Library I have benefited from the kindness of Dr Giles E. Dawson
and Dr James G. McManaway. Of the many other friends who have
come to my assistance, I must mention in particular Professors
William Elton, G. Blakemore Evans, and Richard M. Hosley, Dr
John M. Steadman, and the late Professor John Milton French.
Professor Allardyce Nicoll and Mr George Rylands have kindly
answered my letters of inquiry. My greatest debt is to the General
Editor, whose tolerant exercise of his sharp eye and broad knowledge have made this task an educational as well as a pleasant
experience.

IRVING RIBNER

New Orleans, La.
January 1963

Abbreviations

The following abbreviations are used in the Introduction and Commentary.

(A) WORKS OF REFERENCE, COLLECTED EDITIONS, ETC.

Arber   *A Transcript of the Registers of the Company of Stationers of London*, ed. by Edward Arber (London, 1875–94).

Bentley   G. E. Bentley, *The Jacobean and Caroline Stage* (Oxford, 1941–56).

Bowers   F. T. Bowers, *Elizabethan Revenge Tragedy 1587–1642* (Princeton, 1940).

Brooke   *The Complete Works of Christopher Marlowe*, ed. by C. F. Tucker Brooke (Oxford, 1910).

Brown   John Webster, *The White Devil*, ed. by John Russell Brown [Revels Plays] (London, 1960).

Bullen, *Marston*   *The Works of John Marston*, ed. by A. H. Bullen (London, 1887).

Bullen, *Middleton*   *The Works of Thomas Middleton*, ed. by A. H. Bullen (London, 1885).

Chambers   E. K. Chambers, *The Elizabethan Stage* (Oxford, 1923).

Clarkson and Warren   Paul S. Clarkson and Clyde T. Warren, *The Law of Property in Shakespeare and the Elizabethan Drama* (Baltimore, Md., 1942).

Collins   *The Plays and Poems of Cyril Tourneur*, ed. by John Churton Collins (London, 1878).

Edwards   Thomas Kyd, *The Spanish Tragedy*, ed. by
                       Philip Edwards [Revels Plays] (London, 1959).

Glover and Waller   *The Works of Francis Beaumont and John
                       Fletcher*, ed. by Arnold Glover and A. R.
                       Waller (Cambridge, 1905–12).

Greg, *Bibl.*   W. W. Greg, *A Bibliography of the English
                       Printed Drama to the Restoration* (London,
                       1939–57).

Grierson   *The Poems of John Donne*, ed. by H. J. C. Grier-
                       son (Oxford, 1912).

Herford and   *The Works of Ben Jonson*, ed. by C. H. Herford
   Simpson   and Percy Simpson (Oxford, 1925–52).

Lucas   *The Complete Works of John Webster*, ed. by
                       F. L. Lucas (London, 1927).

McKerrow,   *The Works of Thomas Nashe*, ed. by R. B.
   rev. Wilson   McKerrow, revised by F. P. Wilson (Oxford,
                       1958).

Nicoll   *The Works of Cyril Tourneur*, ed. by Allardyce
                       Nicoll (London [1930]).

O.E.D.   *The Oxford English Dictionary*.

Parrott, *Comedies*   *The Comedies of George Chapman*, ed. by T. M.
                       Parrott (London, 1914).

Parrott, *Tragedies*   *The Tragedies of George Chapman*, ed. by T. M.
                       Parrott (London, 1910).

Partridge   Eric Partridge, *Shakespeare's Bawdy* (London,
                       1947).

Symonds   *Webster and Tourneur*, ed. by J. A. Symonds
                       [Mermaid Series] (London, 1893).

Tilley   M. P. Tilley, *A Dictionary of Proverbs in Eng-
                       land in the Sixteenth and Seventeenth Centuries*
                       (Ann Arbor, Mich., 1950).

Van Fossen   Thomas Heywood, *A Woman Killed with
                       Kindness*, ed. by R. W. Van Fossen [Revels
                       Plays] (London, 1961).

(B) PERIODICALS

J.E.G.P.	*Journal of English and Germanic Philology.*
M.L.N.	*Modern Language Notes.*
M.L.Q.	*Modern Language Quarterly.*
M.L.R.	*Modern Language Review.*
M.P.	*Modern Philology.*
P.M.L.A.	*Publications of the Modern Language Association of America.*
R.E.S.	*Review of English Studies.*
S.P.	*Studies in Philology.*
T.L.S.	*Times Literary Supplement.*

Shakespeare quotations are from the Oxford edition by W. J. Craig.

Introduction

I. CYRIL TOURNEUR AND *THE ATHEIST'S TRAGEDY*

Of Shakespeare's fellow dramatists Cyril Tourneur remains, in spite of the patient research of scholars, among the most shadowy of figures. Indeed, of his career as a dramatist there is little we can say with absolute certainty other than that he was the author of *The Atheist's Tragedy*, for this is the only play published in the seventeenth century to bear his name on its title page. Most scholars have regarded him also as the author of *The Revenger's Tragedy* which was printed anonymously in 1607, since Edward Archer attributed that play to him in the list of plays he appended to *The Old Law* in 1656. Archer was followed in this attribution by Francis Kirkman in his playlists of 1661 (appended to *Tom Tyler and his Wife*) and 1671 (appended to *Nicomede*). But this evidence, in the light of other attributions in these lists, is very shaky, and the play's authorship has long been a subject for controversy, with Thomas Middleton at present perhaps the leading candidate among the sceptics,[1] although Tourneur has had no dearth of champions.[2]

[1] See E. H. C. Oliphant, 'The Authorship of *The Revenger's Tragedy*', *S.P.*, XXIII (1926), 157–68, and *Shakespeare and his Fellow Dramatists* (New York, 1929), II, 93; Samuel Schoenbaum, *Middleton's Tragedies, A Critical Study* (New York, 1955), pp. 156–82; R. H. Barker, *Thomas Middleton* (New York, 1958), pp. 64–75; G. R. Price, 'The Authorship and the Bibliography of *The Revenger's Tragedy*', *The Library*, 5th series, XV (1960), 262–77; and Peter B. Murray, 'The Authorship of "The Revenger's Tragedy"', *Papers of the Bibliographical Society of America*, LVI (1962), 195–218. Professor Schoenbaum in a later study, 'Internal Evidence and the Attribution of Elizabethan Plays', *Bulletin of the N.Y. Public Library*, LXV (1961), 102–24, after a penetrating survey of the entire problem of the attribution of Elizabethan plays, concludes that *The Revenger's Tragedy* can be attributed with certainty neither to Tourneur nor to Middleton and therefore must continue to be regarded as anonymous.

[2] Tourneur's authorship has been defended by H. Dugdale Sykes, *Sidelights on Elizabethan Drama* (London, 1924), p. 221; U. M. Ellis-Fermor,

Tourneur appears also to have been the author of two plays which are no longer extant. The Stationers' Register records that on 15 February 1611/12 there was entered for Edward Blount 'A play booke beinge a Tragecomedye called, The Noble man, written by Cyrill Tourneur',[1] and on 9 September 1653 'The Nobleman, or Great Man, by Cyrill Tourneur' was re-entered by Humphrey Moseley.[2] Whether the play was printed or not we have no way of really knowing, but it is twice mentioned ('The Great Man T' and 'The Nobleman T.C. Cyrill Turnuer') in Warburton's list of plays destroyed by his cook.[3] W. C. Hazlitt wrote of it that 'Dr. Furnivall told me many years ago that the MS. was in the hands of a gentleman at Oxford who was editing Tourneur's works: but I have heard nothing further of it',[4] but of this manuscript no trace has ever been found. We know that the play was acted by the King's Men at court on 23 February 1612 and again at Christmas time in 1612/13,[5] and we have documentary evidence to show that it was still in the repertory of the King's Men on 7 August 1641.[6]

We know also from a letter of 5 June 1613 written by Robert Daborne to Philip Henslowe and preserved among the Henslowe papers at Dulwich College,[7] that Daborne had 'givn Cyrill Tourneur an act of ye Arreignment of London to write.' As both Greg and Nicoll (p. 28) suggest, this is probably to be identified with the lost play, *The Bellman of London*, also mentioned in Henslowe's

'The Imagery of "The Revenger's Tragedie" and "The Atheist's Trage-die"', *M.L.R.*, xxx (1935), 289–301; Harold Jenkins, 'Cyril Tourneur', *R.E.S.*, xvii (1941), 21–36; R. A. Foakes, 'On the Authorship of "The Revenger's Tragedy"', *M.L.R.*, xlviii (1953), 129–38; Inga-Stina Eke-blad, 'On the Authorship of "The Revenger's Tragedy"', *English Studies*, xli (1960), 225–40; and by the present writer in *Jacobean Tragedy* (London, 1962), pp. 72–96. For a comprehensive review of the problem see the forth-coming edition of *The Revenger's Tragedy* in this series by R. A. Foakes.

[1] Greg, *Bibl.*, I, 27.   [2] *Ibid.*, 63.
[3] See W. W. Greg, 'The Bakings of Betsy', *The Library*, 3rd series, II (1911), 225.
[4] *A Manual for the Collector and Amateur of Old English Plays* (London, 1892), p. 167.
[5] Chambers, III, 500, and IV, 126–7.
[6] Bentley, I, 65–6. Nicoll is in error when he writes (p. 25) that 'It is certainly not in the list of King's Men's plays of 1641.'
[7] *Henslowe Papers*, ed. W. W. Greg (London, 1907), pp. 72, 75.

papers, and based probably upon Thomas Dekker's prose pamphlet of that name.

Attempts have been made to attribute some other plays to Tourneur, but for none of these is there any real evidence. Perhaps the strongest case has been made for *The Second Mayden's Tragedy* in BM Lansdowne MS. 807 because of its similarity in plot and atmosphere to *The Revenger's Tragedy*, and since this attribution impinges upon the controversy over that play, Sykes, as might be expected, argues most strongly for Tourneur's authorship, while Oliphant, Schoenbaum, and Barker would assign it to Middleton. Nicoll (pp. 48–9) is perhaps closest to the truth when he suggests that it is more likely by an imitator of *The Revenger's Tragedy* than by the author of that play. Tourneur's hand has been sought also in *The Honest Man's Fortune*, printed in the 1647 Beaumont and Fletcher folio and extant also in a Dyce manuscript at South Kensington,[1] but the stylistic evidence offered in support of this contention is far from convincing.

Indeed, from the meagre facts about Tourneur's life which have come down to us, and which are admirably presented by Nicoll,[2] it seems that Tourneur was a courtier and a soldier whose connection with the theatre was probably a brief and incidental one. We do not know the year of his birth, the year of his death, or where he was educated, but we do know that much of his life was spent in the service of the Vere and Cecil families and that he was engaged abroad for considerable periods of time in military and other affairs. He comes first upon the literary scene with a strange satiric poem,

---

[1] E. H. C. Oliphant, *The Plays of Beaumont and Fletcher* (New Haven, 1927), p. 385; B. M. Wagner in *T.L.S.*, 23 April 1931, p. 327. Dr J. Gerritsen, ed. *The Honest Man's Fortune* (Groningen, 1952), pp. lxviii–lxix, concludes on the basis of elaborate language and verse tests that Tourneur must have been the author of the first four scenes of Act I, suggesting that 'it may perhaps not be thought unfitting that the author of *The Honest Man's Revenge*, as the sub-title of *The Atheist's Tragedie* runs, should have had a hand in *The Honest Man's Fortune*' (p. xci).

[2] The only significant addition that may be made to Nicoll's account of Tourneur's life is contained in a letter to *T.L.S.* for 16 April 1931, p. 301, by J. R. Sutherland, who cites a letter written from Nijmegen on 14 August 1614 which establishes beyond doubt that Tourneur saw military action in the Low Countries and that he spent time in the service of the Vere family, as had already been supposed on the basis of other evidence.

full of obscure allegory, called *The Transformed Metamorphosis*, published in 1600, although probably written some year or two earlier, and strongly influenced by the satires of John Marston then much in vogue. He may have been the author also of a black-letter prose pamphlet called *Laugh and lie downe: or, The Worldes Folly*, printed in 1605 by Jeffrey Charlton, the one extant copy of which now survives in the Huntington Library, although there is little evidence of his authorship other than the initials 'C. T.' appended to the dedication.[1]

Largely because of his association with the Vere family Tourneur has been credited with *A Funerall Poeme Upon the Death of the Most Worthie And True Souldier, Sir Francis Vere* which was entered in the Stationers' Register on 16 October 1609[2] and printed in quarto in the same year. Although no name appears on the title page of this edition, Tourneur's authorship has never seriously been questioned. Also stemming from his patronage in high places may be the *Character of Robert Earl of Salisbury* which Tourneur prepared soon after the death of Robert Cecil on 24 May 1612.[3] Within a brief period following this, Tourneur must have completed his *A Griefe on the Death of Prince Henrie*, which was entered in the Stationers' Register on 25 December 1612 as by 'Cirill Turnour'[4] and printed early in 1613 in *Three Elegies on the most lamented Death of Prince Henrie*. The other two elegists were John Webster and Thomas Heywood, and for each poem a separate title page was printed bearing the author's name. One of the two Huntington Library copies of this volume contains an eight-line poem 'On the Succession', signed 'C. T.', which was evidently suppressed during the course of printing. To this list of Tourneur's writings two brief additions may be made.[5] The one is a six-line poem 'On the death of a child but one year old', first printed by

---

[1] Nicoll (pp. 17–18) concludes that 'no positive assertion is made, or can be made, concerning his participation in its writing'.

[2] Arber, III, 419.

[3] Nicoll reprints two of five manuscript versions of this prose character known to him, that in BM Harleian MS. 36 and that at Clifton Hall, Nottingham. B. M. Wagner in *T.L.S.*, 23 April 1931, p. 327, calls attention to a sixth MS. in the Bodleian, containing a clear signature, 'Cyrill Tourneur', which may well be authentic.

[4] Arber, III, 510.   [5] Cf. B. M. Wagner, *T.L.S.*, 18 Sept. 1933, p. 651.

A. B. Grosart[1] and signed 'Cecill Turner', coupling Tourneur's
name with that of the family he served. The other, signed 'C. T.',
is a poem of eight seven-line stanzas called 'Of my Lady Anne
Cecill, the Lord Burleigh's Daughter', attesting again to Tourneur's connections with the Cecil family. It was printed in 'A col-
lection of Several Ingenious Poems and Songs', added to *Le Prince
D'Amour* (1660).

Our knowledge of *The Atheist's Tragedy* is as fragmentary as our
knowledge of its author's career. It was entered in the Stationers'
Register on 14 September 1611 for John Stepneth as 'A booke
called, The Tragedy of the Atheist',[2] and it was printed later in the
same year, with the title page informing us that 'in diuers places it
hath often beene Acted.' There are no contemporary references to
it of any kind, and in what 'diuers places' it was acted we have no
way of knowing. It has been suggested[3] that the title page statement
would indicate that the play was not produced by an important
company at a well-known theatre such as the Globe or Blackfriars,
since such information was usually stated proudly on title pages,
and that it may therefore have been produced by some minor company in the provinces. Of its later stage history we know equally
little, for there seem to be no records of its ever having been performed anywhere. It seems to have been admired by John Genest,
who says of it only that 'the part of D'Amville would just have
suited Kean.'[4]

2. DATE

Early historians of the drama regarded *The Atheist's Tragedy* as the
earlier of Tourneur's two extant plays, and thus they dated it well
before 7 October 1607, when *The Revenger's Tragedy* was entered
in the Stationers' Register.[5] F. G. Fleay,[6] for instance, held that it
must have been written some time before the end of the siege of

---

[1] 'Literary Finds in Trinity College, Dublin and Elsewhere', *Englische
Studien*, XXVI (1899), 16–17.

[2] Greg, *Bibl.*, I, 27.

[3] T. M. Parrott and R. H. Ball, *A Short View of Elizabethan Drama*
(New York, 1958), p. 213.

[4] *Some Account of the English Stage* (Bath, 1832), X, 21.

[5] Greg, *Bibl.*, I, 23.

[6] *A Biographical Chronicle of the English Drama* (London, 1891), II, 263.

Ostend, which lasted from 1601 to 1604, for the lengthy account of
it (II. i. 40–94) to have meant very much to a contemporary audience, and F. E. Schelling[1] confidently asserted, without offering
evidence of any kind, that 'it seems almost certainly to have been
acted in 1602 or 1603'. Levin Schucking,[2] following Fleay, suggested that the 'certain great man' of I. ii. 108 ff. was Sir Francis
Vere, that the passage referred to his illness of August 1602, and
that the play must therefore be dated in the winter of 1602/3. To
this view of *The Atheist's Tragedy* as the earlier of Tourneur's plays,
Collins (I, xxxii) also subscribed.

More recent writers have recognized that while *The Revenger's
Tragedy* may be the greater artistic achievement, this does not mean
that it was necessarily later in time of composition. The reference
to the siege of Ostend merely dates the time of the play's action and
proves that it was written some time after 1601. Of somewhat
greater value as evidence is the close relation between *The Atheist's
Tragedy* and the mature tragedies of Shakespeare, notably *King
Lear*,[3] which would make late 1606 or early 1607 the earliest possible limit.[4] The highly polemic tone of the play suggests, moreover, that it was written in reply to some other play, and H. H.
Adams has argued that this play was Chapman's *Revenge of Bussy
D'Ambois*, which could not have been written much earlier than
1610, Tourneur seeking in his play to offer an orthodox Christian
reply to Chapman's Senecan Stoicism.[5] Although not agreeing entirely with Adams on the terms of the relationship of Tourneur's
play to *The Revenge*, Clifford Leech has held that *The Atheist's
Tragedy* was designed as a dramatic comment not only on that play,
but on Chapman's earlier *Bussy D'Ambois* (ca. 1603) as well, even
the name 'D'Ambois' being echoed in 'D'Amville' as 'Clermont' is
echoed in 'Charlemont', and Bussy providing the point of depar-
ture for Tourneur's imagining of his supreme atheist.[6] These argu-

---

[1] *Elizabethan Drama 1558–1642* (Boston, 1908), I, 564.

[2] 'Eine Anleihe Shakespeares bei Tourneur', *Englische Studien*, L (1916–
17), 95–6.

[3] Cf. below, pp. lxiii–lxvi.   [4] Chambers, III, 499.

[5] 'Cyril Tourneur on Revenge', *J.E.G.P.*, XLVIII (1949), 82–6.

[6] '*The Atheist's Tragedy* as a Dramatic Comment on Chapman's *Bussy*
Plays', *J.E.G.P.*, LII (1953), 525–30.

ments are well taken, and it would appear most likely that, as E. E. Stoll suggested many years ago,[1] *The Atheist's Tragedy* belongs to the year 1611, having been completed very soon before its entry in the Stationers' Register on 14 September of that year.

3. THE TEXT

The Atheist's Tragedy was printed in quarto in 1611 with the following title page:

THE / ATHEIST'S / TRAGEDIE: / *OR* / The honest Man's Reuenge. / *As in diuers places it hath often beene acted.* / [line] WRITTEN / By *Cyril Tourneur*. / [line, ornament] *AT LONDON*, / Printed for *Iohn Stepneth*, and *Richard Redmer*, and are to / be sold at their Shops at the West end of Paules. / 1611.

Some uncorrected copies of this quarto (Huntington Bridgewater 1612, and BM C.12.f.8) read '*Stepney*', and '*Redmere*'. Some of the same sheets were issued with a variant date of 1612 on the title pages, the two issues being identical in all other respects.

The collation is A[1], B–K[4], L[3]. A[1], comprising the title page and 'The names and qualities of the Actors', is in actuality L[4] transferred to the beginning of the book. Copies of the quarto are fairly numerous. Of those bearing the 1611 imprint there are three in the British Museum, three in the Huntington Library, and one at each of the following libraries: Bodleian, Eton, Worcester College Oxford, Boston Public, Congress, Folger, Newberry, Texas, Yale, and Harvard. Of those bearing the 1612 imprint there is one copy at each of the following libraries: the Dyce and Forster collections at South Kensington, British Museum, Harvard, Huntington, and Folger. The present edition is based upon a photostatic reproduction of the Dyce copy at South Kensington which has been collated with all thirteen copies in the United States. The General Editor has kindly checked some readings for me in the four British Museum copies.

---

[1] *John Webster* (Boston, 1905), pp. 210–13. 'We may, I think', writes Nicoll (p. 23) also, 'lacking other proof, assume that *The Atheist's Tragedy* appeared on the stage about 1610 or 1611.'

The quarto is carefully divided into five acts, each set off with carefully correct Latin (i.e., Actus primi Scena prima), but it contains no scene division. In the present edition the scene divisions indicated marginally in square brackets are those established by John Churton Collins and followed by Allardyce Nicoll. Otherwise, the quarto is followed very closely, for it is a very carefully printed one which presents few editorial problems. Exits and entrances are accurately and clearly indicated, and stage directions are usually so full and descriptive as to suggest to at least one scholar that 'the inevitable inference from a careful examination of this text is that Tourneur himself prepared for a reading public the manuscript which became the printer's copy'.[1] Stage directions which are clearly authorial include those at I. ii. 191.1, I. iii. 0.1, II. ii. 17.1–2, II. v. 0.1, II. vi. 67.1, III. i. 0.1, III. i. 6.1–2, III. i. 52.1, III. ii. 17.1–2, III. iii. 0.1, III. iv. 54.1, IV. iii. 0.1–2, IV. iii. 34.1–2, IV. iii. 70.1–3, IV. iii. 77.1–2, IV. iii. 204.1–2, IV. iii. 210.1–2, IV. iv. 14.1, IV. v. 0.1, and IV. v. 60.1.

The extraordinarily large number of verse passages which have been set as prose, however, makes it difficult to believe that the play could have been set directly from an author's holograph. Since many of these passages are in the speeches of D'Amville or those in conversation with him, Nicoll conjectured (p. 322) that D'Amville's role may have been revised before the manuscript was taken to the printers, but this supposition, although possible, is not sufficient to account for the great number of such passages in a text which otherwise gives evidence of having been printed with great care. It is possible also that the compositor was anxious to save space, but a more plausible explanation may be that the play was printed from a scribal fair copy of Tourneur's holograph rather than from the holograph itself, and that the copyist had little compunction about transcribing verse as prose.

There are in the quarto few of the usual signs of theatrical use such as anticipated entrances, but in addition to its large share of authorial stage directions the quarto does contain some directions which are clearly not authorial, such for instance as that at II. i.

[1] G. R. Price, 'The Authorship and Bibliography of *The Revenger's Tragedy*', *The Library*, 5th series, xv (1960), 264.

106.1, being almost certainly prompter's memoranda.[1] It is difficult
to come to any certain conclusions about the provenance of the
quarto, but one not impossible hypothesis may be that a fair copy of
Tourneur's manuscript, not itself prepared for use in the theatre,
was used as a prompt-copy by some provincial company, and that
this manuscript, with the prompter's additions to Tourneur's directions, provided the copy for the quarto. The printing must have
been done with great care, and the unusually careful proof-reading
which the text seems to have undergone[2] raises the intriguing possi-
bility that the printing may have been supervised by Tourneur
himself.

The punctuation of the quarto is very careful by Jacobean standards, the intention of the author being almost always obvious. It
is rather heavy and emphatic, with a tendency to set off subordinate
clauses and mere phrases as sentences, and it frequently uses exclamation marks after vocatives, where mere commas would ordi-
narily be called for. As is common in Jacobean texts, the question
mark is used freely for the exclamation point. Punctuation has been
lightened considerably in this edition, in accordance with modern
usage, by the removal of unnecessary stops and by the substitution
in many places of commas for semi-colons and colons where only
slight pauses are called for. In the few instances where departures
from the quarto punctuation may involve a questionable interpretation of the author's intention with regard to rhetorical pause or
nuance of meaning, these changes are noted in the collation.

Because of their unusual fullness, stage directions have had to be
modified very infrequently in the present text, and such modifica-
tion is indicated in the collation notes, with additions to the quarto
enclosed within square brackets. Spelling has been modernized
throughout, and where modern forms have been substituted for
archaic words which are not mere spelling variations such changes
are noted in the collation. In rearranging passages falsely printed
as verse, and in correcting the few other instances of mislineation
in the text, I have generally, though not always, followed the prac-

[1] See W. J. Lawrence, *Pre-Restoration Stage Studies* (Cambridge, Mass.,
1927), pp. 131–2.
[2] Cf. below, pp. xxviii–xxix.

tice of Nicoll. Since these departures from the quarto lineation are fairly numerous, I have thought it best to list them all together in an appendix.

A comparison of fourteen copies of the quarto reveals that the text underwent some correction during the course of impression, much of it on sheet K. Most of the variants are simple corrections of obvious errors. One passage, however, may be of some bibliographical interest, for it appears in three different states and may provide some insight into proof-reading practice. The passage occurs on sig. B4^v (I. ii. 103–5). In one copy (Newberry) it appears as follows:

> *Lang.* I salute you both with the spirit of copulation,
>   I am already informed of your matrimoniall
>   Purposes, and will be a testimonie to the integritie.

This attempt to make poetry out of prose is corrected in some other copies (Huntington Hoe 1611, Harvard 1612, Folger 1611, BM C.34.e.10, BM 1077.k.5, the BM copy dated 1612, and Forster) so that it reads as follows:

> *Lang.* I salute you both with the spirit of copulation, I am already informed of your matrimoniall purposes, and will be a testimonie to the integritie.

The proof-reader, evidently noting that the passage should be in prose, moved 'I am' from the second to the first line and moved 'Purposes, and will be a' from the third to the second, substituting a lower case 'p' in 'purposes', but otherwise retaining the old type. In all of these copies, the final words of the first two lines, 'I am' and 'be a', are badly blurred, in some cases (Harvard 1612 and BM C.34.e.10) almost invisible. This may be because the shifting of type created an unevenness in the bed which made it impossible for the words to take ink properly.[1] The proof-reader must then have noticed that the passage was still incorrect. He added the three missing words to the final line and eliminated the cause of the blurring, making the passage read as it appears in all other copies:

> *Lang.* I salute you both with the spirit of copulation, I am already informed of your matrimoniall purposes, and will be a testimonie to the integritie of your promises.

[1] I owe this explanation to Dr Giles E. Dawson of the Folger Library.

This kind of careful proof-reading, not common in Elizabethan dramatic texts—particularly the restoration to prose of a falsely versified speech—may perhaps indicate that the printing was supervised by Tourneur himself.

The Atheist's Tragedy was never included in any of the eighteenth- or nineteenth-century collections of plays, although it was reprinted separately by T. Wilkins in 1792 and again in 1794. The first modern edition is that of John Churton Collins, *The Plays and Poems of Cyril Tourneur* (London, 1878), where the play appears in the first of two volumes. This is a very careless edition, with words omitted, and with many unexplainable departures from the quarto. Collins made no attempt to collate different copies of the quarto, and this was particularly unfortunate because he appears to have used one of the largely uncorrected copies, probably BM C.34.e.10 or BM 1077.k.5, since he reproduces errors common to these copies. John Addington Symonds included the play in his Mermaid edition, *Webster and Tourneur* (London, 1893), basing his text closely on that of Collins, from which he departs only to the extent of modernizing spelling and punctuation. All of Collins's errors are perpetuated. The play is included also in *The Works of Cyril Tourneur*, edited by Allardyce Nicoll (London, [1930]), the most reliable edition which has appeared thus far. Nicoll collated the four British Museum copies, the Dyce, Forster, and Bodleian copies, and he examined photostats of some pages of the Huntington Library copies. His failure to check the other American copies caused him to miss some variants, however. Nicoll's is an old spelling text which follows the quarto with great fidelity, and to it I am much indebted.

4. SOURCES

For the main plot of *The Atheist's Tragedy* no source has been discovered, but it is not unlikely that the events may be based upon some murder story which Tourneur read, possibly in the French or Italian, although the roles of the principal characters are carefully shaped in the manner of allegory to illustrate moral principles. Collins (p. xxiv) writes that 'The plot, or rather the series of melodramatic incidents which usurps its name, is obviously original, though it is possible that the germ of it may be lurking somewhere in contemporary French records. A cursory glance through Thuanus, Mezerai, and Jean de Serres has, however, led to nothing.'

Gerard Langbaine[1] was probably the first to suggest that one incident in the play, Levidulcia's manner of getting Fresco and Sebastian out of her chamber when she is surprised by her husband (II. v), has its origins in the sixth novel of the seventh day of Boccaccio's *Decameron*. Since the earliest English translation of the *Decameron* was that printed by Isaac Jaggard in 1620, if Tourneur used Boccaccio he must have read the tale in the Italian or in one of the many French translations available.[2] But Tourneur need not have gone directly to Boccaccio's story of Isabella, Leonetto, and Lambertuccio, for the story is widespread in continental folklore,[3] and several versions of the incident had appeared in English collections as well. The account of a lady who in the same manner gets rid of two lovers when surprised by her husband appears as 'Why the Gentlewoman of Lyons sat with her haire clipt off in Purgatory' in *Tarletons Newes out of Purgatorie* (1590) [Sig. F1ᵛ–F3ᵛ]. The story is told again 'as it is recorded by two Florentines, who have written of it almost in the same manner' in *A World of Wonders* (1607) [Sig. K6ʳ],[4] the two Florentines being presumably Boccaccio and Sansovino. This version, or more likely the French version of

---

[1] *An Account of the English Dramatick Poets* (Oxford, 1691), p. 505. See also Emil Koeppel, *Quellen-Studien zu den Dramen Ben Jonson's, John Marston's und Beaumont und Fletcher's* (Erlangen and Leipzig, 1895), pp. 137–8.

[2] The French translation of Laurent de Premierfait, completed in 1414, was printed by Antoine Verard in 1485 and had gone through eight editions by 1541. The more accurate rendition by Antoine le Macon appeared in 1545 and by 1615 had gone through nineteen editions. See Herbert G. Wright, *Boccaccio in England from Chaucer to Tennyson* (London, 1957), p. 113. I am indebted to Wright, *passim*, for references to versions of the tale which follow.

[3] Joseph Bedier, *Les Fabliaux* (Paris, 1925), pp. 229–36, calls attention to the French fabliau *Lai d'Épervier*, which is essentially Boccaccio's tale, and to various versions in Sanskrit, Arabic, and in the *Gesta Romanorum*. The story appears also as number 266 of the *Facezie* (ca. 1480) of Poggio Bracciolini and as the tenth novella of the third day of Francesco Sansovino's *Cento Novelle Scelte* (Venice, 1571) [Sig. K1ᵛ–K3ʳ].

[4] This work was a translation of Henri Estienne, *L'Introduction au traité de la conformité des merueilles anciennes auec les modernes* (1566).

which it is a translation, may have been the source of Samuel Row-
lands's satiric portrait of 'A Cuckold' in *The Knave of Clubbes* (1609)
[Sig. D4^v–E3^r] where we have the same set of events.[1]

Boccaccio's essential situation occurs also in Act II, scene vi, of
Beaumont and Fletcher's *Women Pleased*, but that Tourneur could
have known this play is not likely, for it cannot be dated before
1619,[2] although it is possible that an earlier version of the play,
either by Beaumont and Fletcher or some other authors, may have
existed as early as 1603 or 1604.[3] It would have been possible, however, for Tourneur to read the version of the incident which appears
in Edward Sharpham's play, *Cupid's Whirligig*, which was entered
in the Stationers' Register for John Busbye and Arthur Johnson on
29 June 1607[4] and printed by Edward Allde in the same year. In
Sharpham's version [Sig. H3^v–I2^r] the lovers are a cowardly Captain Wouldly and a Master Exhibition of the Inns of Court who
speaks in legal jargon. The captain corresponds to Tourneur's
Fresco and the lawyer to his Sebastian. Tourneur's version corresponds more closely to those in *A World of Wonders* and *The Knave
of Clubbes* than it does to Sharpham's, in which the heroine is actually a chaste wife tormented by a jealous husband and anxious to be
rid of her two ludicrous and unwelcome suitors.

Still another version of the incident appears in the jig of 'Singing
Simpkin', first printed in Robert Cox's *Acteon and Diana* (1656)
[Sig. C2^r–D1^r].[5] It has been argued[6] that this version in spite of its
late printing, is of Elizabethan origin and was Tourneur's immediate source. But the similarities of the jig to Tourneur's scene are not
so striking as Cope would suppose, and with the many versions of
the story we know to have been extant, to suggest this as the imme-

---

[1] This work was first printed, as Wright points out, as *Tis Merry When
Knaves Meet*, of which no copy appears to be extant, and thus may have
been too early to have been based on the 1607 translation of Estienne.

[2] Bentley, III, 431–2.

[3] Cf. E. H. C. Oliphant, *The Plays of Beaumont and Fletcher* (New
Haven, Conn., 1927), pp. 156–9.

[4] Greg, *Bibl.*, I, 23.

[5] See C. R. Baskervill, *The Elizabethan Jig* (Chicago, 1929), pp. 235–8.
The jig is reprinted on pp. 444–9.

[6] J. I. Cope, 'Tourneur's *Atheist's Tragedy* and the Jig of "Singing
Simpkin"', *M.L.N.*, LXX (1955), 571–3.

diate source—and thus to suggest a close relation between Tourneur and an oral tradition of popular entertainment—would be
extremely hazardous.

It has been suggested also[1] that the disguised Borachio's description of the siege of Ostend (II. i. 40–94) may owe something to *The
Commentaries of Sir Francis Vere* which, after lying in manuscript
for many years, was published at Oxford in 1657. It is quite possible
that Tourneur may have seen this work before its publication, for
he was in the service of the Vere family, and he may have consulted
it when writing his funeral elegy on Sir Francis in 1609.[2] But, by
the same token, Tourneur himself was almost certainly at the siege
in the general's service and had no need to rely upon his patron's
reminiscences. Collins has noted some 'little points and particulars
which Tourneur has seized' from Vere's account, but the parallels
are not close enough to amount to much as evidence. Nor is it
possible to detect verbal borrowings from *A True Historie of the
Memorable Siege of Ostend*, published in London in 1604.

5. THE PLAY

a. Tourneur's Morality and the Critics

Criticism of Tourneur has tended to concentrate upon *The Revenger's Tragedy*, understandably perhaps, for that is the greater artistic achievement. But *The Atheist's Tragedy* has considerable merit
of its own, and it occupies a historical position which makes it
worthy of study. There is no play quite like it in the entire Jacobean
repertory, and as has been argued recently with great cogency,[3] an
understanding of *The Atheist's Tragedy* may do much to illuminate
Tourneur's greater play for us and to confirm his common authorship of both. This view of a close thematic relation between the two
plays is a fairly recent one.[4] Most critics have tended to emphasize
instead the disparity of the plays in theme as well as technique,[5] and

[1] Collins, I, 158.   [2] Cf. above, p. xxii.

[3] John Peter, *Complaint and Satire in Early English Literature* (Oxford,
1956), pp. 255–87.

[4] It was argued effectively for perhaps the first time by Harold Jenkins
in *R.E.S.*, XVII (1941), 21–36.

[5] The older view survives in Robert Ornstein, *The Moral Vision of
Jacobean Tragedy* (Madison, Wis., 1960), where the supposed incompati-

thus, even while they supported Tourneur's authorship of both, to lend force to the challenging of his claim to the greater one.

The merit of Tourneur, as earlier critics viewed him, and as some continue to view him today, lay in his ability to evoke a poetic vision of a world so corrupt and vitiated by evil as to leave no hope for humanity. The gothic horror of this conception *The Revenger's Tragedy* was seen as expressing perfectly, with *The Atheist's Tragedy* viewed usually by those who accepted his authorship of both plays as appending an unconvincing moral lesson to a narrower and more circumscribed view of essentially the same world.[1] It was for the amazing unity of his poetic incarnation of evil that Swinburne celebrated Tourneur as one whose language

> would recall the passion and the perfection, the fervour and the splendour and the harmony, which even we at this distance of time, and through the twilight of a dead language, can recognize in the dialogue or the declamation of Æschylus himself.[2]

For Swinburne, Tourneur was the poet of such moral fervour that he could regard the world only with a savage indignation expressing itself in sublime poetry. But poetry which expressed only a loathing for humanity, although the product of moral indignation, could not itself embody a consistent moral vision, and A. H. Thorndike,[3] viewing *The Revenger's Tragedy* in Swinburne's terms, could write that 'it is governed by a sheer delight in horror and unrelieved by any moral standard'. A similar belief in the essential amorality of Tourneur led T. S. Eliot[4] to write that *The Revenger's Tragedy*

---

bility of the two plays is thus explained: 'We need not posit, then, that Tourneur experienced a religious "conversion" between *The Revenger's Tragedy* (1607) and *The Atheist's Tragedy* (1611). More than likely the latter play simply chronicles a return to orthodoxy that was Tourneur's fundamental position after a temporary disillusionment which he immortalized in Italianate metaphor' (p. 118).

[1] Cf. U. M. Ellis-Fermor, *The Jacobean Drama* (London, 1936), pp. 153–69.

[2] *Contemporaries of Shakespeare*, ed. E. Gosse and T. J. Wise (London, 1919), p. 177. Cf. also *The Age of Shakespeare* (London, 1908), pp. 259–86.

[3] *Tragedy* (Boston, 1908), p. 202.

[4] *Selected Essays 1917–1932* (London, 1932), p. 189. Madeleine Doran, *Endeavors of Art* (Madison, Wis., 1954), finds also in Tourneur an 'ambiguity of ethical implication' (p. 354) and concludes that 'Tourneur is not really interested in how a man may be drawn into doing wrong to right wrong,

achieves its 'amazing unity' by its ability to express 'an intense and unique and horrible vision of life; but [it] is such a vision as might come, as the result of few or slender experiences, to a highly sensitive adolescent with a gift for words'. Of *The Atheist's Tragedy* he could only say, while admitting that it was the later play, that 'it adds nothing at all to what the other play has given us; there is no development, no fresh inspiration; only the skilful but uninspired use of a greater metrical variety'.

Much of the argument for the moral inadequacy of Tourneur has sprung from an equation of the author with his principal characters, as when J. A. Bastiaenen[1] writes:

> Tourneur also does not think much of religion. A more materialistic way of rejecting all expectation of a life to come in favor of a lustful epicurean career than occurs at the beginning of *The Atheist's Tragedy* it would be difficult to conceive. The free and easy manner in which man is lowered to the level of the beast is repulsive. However, it should not be forgotten that the persons concerned are utter scoundrels.

And while he recognizes that Tourneur himself may have had some moral purpose in giving such views to scoundrels, his general estimate is that 'whatever moral purpose the author may have had in view when depicting characters of this description, perversity like this ought not to have been brought on the stage'.[2]

Those critics who have regarded Tourneur's plays as most deficient in moral vision, even while praising the brilliance of their poetry—as though such a separation could be made—are those who have failed to see them, as Peter has shown that they must be seen, in terms of a long tradition of medieval homiletic and hortatory

---

that is with the fundamental tragic problem that revenge raises, but simply in the mordant depiction of a vicious and ugly world; if so, revenge for him may be just a technique for making a play' (p. 354). So also M. E. Prior, *The Language of Tragedy* (New York, 1947), pp. 135–6, sees Tourneur as having limited his genius by a mere reworking of the 'ready made popular dramatic convention' of revenge tragedy. T. M. Tomlinson, 'The Morality of Revenge: Tourneur's Critics', *Essays in Criticism*, x (1960), 134–47, finds also a moral ambivalence in Tourneur, after surveying the attempts of Peter and others to support a contrary view.

[1] *The Moral Tone of Jacobean and Caroline Drama* (Amsterdam, 1930), p. 177.

[2] *Ibid.*, p. 82.

literature. Tourneur is, in fact, among the most rigidly moralistic
dramatists of his day, embodying in his work a primitive Christian-   *Ribner!*
ity, and for this reason using the non-naturalistic allegorical method
of medieval literature, filling his plays with symbols which had been
used traditionally to preach a contempt for the things of this world
in expectation of the joys of heaven.[1] Probably because William
Archer found it difficult to view drama other than in terms of nineteenth-century naturalism, he was led to call *The Revenger's Tragedy* 'the work of a sanguinary maniac who cannot even write toler-
able verse',[2] and to conclude that 'not the least nauseous feature of
Tourneur's work—and he shares it with many of his contemporaries—is the pose of indignant morality under which he tries to dissemble his gloating appetite for horrors'.[3]

If seen in terms of a moral *exemplum* by which Tourneur seeks to
embody certain Christian principles similar to those he had expressed by more subtle poetic means in his earlier play, the structure and meaning of *The Atheist's Tragedy* are very clear, and what
otherwise might appear as a play about mechanical, lifeless characters involved in absurd situations comes to have some artistic merit
in terms of its own dramatic medium. The difference between
Tourneur's two plays is not one so much of moral viewpoint as it
is of dramatic method. In *The Atheist's Tragedy*, as one recent critic
has written,[4]

> we are asked to follow an argument which eventually proves
> D'Amville to be wrong and damned; in *The Revenger's Tragedy*
> we are asked for immediate responses to the evils that are being
> demonstrated, through the swiftly moving intrigue which hurries
> us from one striking situation to another, and through out-of-plot
> speeches.

D'Amville in his own way is a tragic hero, but his tragedy lies not,
as in Shakespeare's *Macbeth*, for instance, in the decline and damnation of a believable fellow human being in whom, in spite of his
villainy, we can see the reflection of our own human condition. It

---

[1] On Tourneur's medievalism, see also L. G. Salingar, ' "The Revenger's
Tragedy" and the Morality Tradition', *Scrutiny*, VI (1938), 402–22.
[2] *The Old Drama and the New* (London, 1923), p. 73.   [3] *Ibid.*, p. 75.
[4] Inga-Stina Ekeblad, 'An Approach to Tourneur's Imagery', *M.L.R.*,
LIV (1959), 496.

lies rather in the refutation of an intellectual proposition of which
the hero is a dramatic symbol. If Tourneur does not always appear
entirely hostile to D'Amville, and if D'Amville has a greater charm
and vitality than the virtuous Charlemont, this is not to be taken as
evidence of moral ambiguity on the author's part. It was traditional
in English drama from the time of the Miracle and Morality plays
to stress the attractive side of vice; one need only consider the wit
and charm of Shakespeare's Richard III. If the play is to be the
tragedy of D'Amville (the man egregiously mistaken), as much as
it is an illustration of the Christian virtue of Charlemont and Castabella, we cannot be without some feeling of value in the figure
whose downfall we behold. Tourneur must also prepare his audience for the final understanding which comes to D'Amville and the
consequent reformation which is part of his tragic progression.

Herschel Baker[1] reflects a common point of view when he de-
scribes Charlemont as

> the *reductio ad absurdum* of the Stoic hero: he accepts the universe,
> but his acquiescence is indistinguishable from a tearful Christian
> sentimentality; his resignation reflects less of a philosophic policy
> than an incapacity for action, and he seems to be the death wish
> made articulate.

When Charlemont is seen in realistic terms and judged as we would
a fellow mortal, this appears to be true, but within the play's frame
of reference it is grossly unfair. We cannot compare Charlemont to
Hamlet; Tourneur's patient man has meaning only as an antithesis
to the intellectual position of D'Amville. As the embodiment of an
orthodox Christian proposition which is from beginning to end
firm and unchanging, he acquires a rigidity which makes his conduct border on the absurd.[2] Naturalistic critics have been disturbed
by the absolutes of good and evil in Tourneur, the virtues of Charlemont and Castabella being so perfect that the characters seem lifeless and unbelievable puppets, just as D'Amville and Levidulcia,
by the monstrousness of their bestiality, appear incredible. This

---

[1] *The Wars of Truth* (London, 1952), p. 113.

[2] Critics, in a similar manner, have censured Shakespeare's Edgar in
King Lear as lacking in vitality when compared with Edmund, but this is
not to be taken as evidence of moral ambiguity on Shakespeare's part. It
may have been a consequence of the thematic structure of the play.

has been offered as evidence of a strong Calvinist strain in Tourneur's work,[1] which involves a rigid separation between the great
majority of the damned and the few elect. But this rigidity is perhaps more surely the result of Tourneur's allegorical method. He is
dealing in absolutes, and his intellectual propositions are presented
in the clearest and least ambiguous terms, with a kind of exaggera-
tion common to moral *exempla*.

It is unfortunate that criticism of *The Atheist's Tragedy* must
stem entirely from the reading of the play rather than from stage
performance. Since there has been no known revival of the work—
indeed no record of any performances other than those of uncertain
locale referred to on the title page—we have no evidence of how the
play may have appeared to a theatre audience at any time in history.
Only when it is subjected to the test of actual performance will we
ever really be able to judge the effectiveness of Tourneur's distinctive dramatic technique.

b. Theme and Structure[2]

The Atheist's Tragedy is built upon a conflict between two dia-
metrically opposed conceptions of man's position in the universe
and between the ethical systems entailed by these conceptions. On
the one hand we have the atheism of D'Amville, a creed arrived at
by fallible human reason, which sees physical nature as the ultimate
power in the universe, governed by its own fixed and mechanical
laws of cause and effect, uncontrolled by any supernatural influ-
ences. Opposed to this is the religion of Charlemont, based upon
faith in a supreme being superior to physical nature of which He is
always master, governing mankind with justice as well as mercy.
D'Amville's creed expresses itself in a view of man as animal, unable to escape the physical laws of nature which bind him to all
other animals, and in a lust for self-gratification and power at no
matter what cost to other men. That of Charlemont appears in a
Christian patience which enables him to accept whatever suffering

[1] Cf. M. H. Higgins, 'The Influence of Calvinistic Thought in Tourneur's *Atheist's Tragedy*', *R.E.S.*, xix (1943), 255–62.
[2] Much of this section is based on my *Jacobean Tragedy: The Quest for
Moral Order* (London, 1962), pp. 86–96.

the providential order of the universe may decree and leads him to acts of love and charity as the pathways to salvation, the highest goal of man. The action of the play comes thus to consist of two parallel movements, the one devoted to a systematic refutation of D'Amville's creed and a demonstration of the falseness of his view of human felicity, the other to a demonstration of Charlemont's way as the only one which can assure man's happiness on earth as well as in heaven. Both points are made by the final axe stroke which knocks out D'Amville's brains, not to be regarded as a ludicrous accident by which a simple-minded dramatist resolves his plot, but rather as a miracle, deliberately chosen for its apparent impossibility, by which Tourneur emphasizes the intervention of God to destroy the wicked and protect the innocent.

It has been shown that the creed which D'Amville proclaims throughout the play is a composite of what Tourneur's contemporaries generally believed to be the beliefs of atheists, gathered by the author out of various books devoted to the refutation of atheism.[1] Although the word 'atheist' was very loosely used and could be applied to almost any unpopular shade of belief, it included most commonly the separation of belief in nature from belief in God, and a confidence in the power of man to live by the rules of nature rather than those of revealed religion. To the orthodox Christian there could be no such separation, for to live by nature was to live in accordance with the divine plan of God who had created nature, and human reason, if not perverted, could only lead man to a faith in God. This view of the relation of nature to God is well expressed by Guillaume du Vair,[2] one of the most widely read of continental moralists:

[1] Robert Ornstein, '*The Atheist's Tragedy* and Renaissance Naturalism', *S.P.*, LI (1954), 194–207. For perhaps the best account of Renaissance notions of atheism, see E. A. Strathmann, 'Elizabethan Meanings of Atheism', in *Sir Walter Ralegh: A Study in Elizabethan Skepticism* (New York, 1951), pp. 61–97. Cf. also G. T. Buckley, *Atheism in the English Renaissance* (Chicago, 1932); Paul H. Kocher, *Science and Religion in Elizabethan England* (San Marino, Calif., 1953).

[2] *A Buckler Against Adversitie: or a Treatise of Constancie*, tr. by Andrew Court (1622) [Sig. S1ᵛ]. This attitude is characteristic of Renaissance neo-stoicism which continued the Christianization of stoic philosophy begun in the Middle Ages. For the mechanical natural laws which for classical

For I doubt not, but in the creation of this Vniverse, God hath established a rule and a certaine Law, whereby all things must be produced, disposed of, and maintained, which if any one will call Nature, I will not gainesay, so that he makes not of it an Essence separated from God: vnto the which hee should thinke hee had committed the gouernment of things created to set himselfe on rest. Contrariwise, this Nature can bee nothing else but the first Power and Vertue, which from the beginning, without any separation from him, hath printed it selfe in the matter, and hath giuen vnto it that regular motion by which things are maintained in their being, and bring foorth their effects besides.

D'Amville stands, on the contrary, for Renaissance scepticism, and his creation reflects the fear and horror with which some conservative minds viewed the growth of a new empirical science and the challenging of traditional values of order and degree.

It was believed that, since the atheist recognized no supernatural power in the universe, he could know none of those feelings of love, loyalty, kindness, gratitude, and the like which Renaissance moralists held to be emanations on the human plane of the love of God which ruled the universe. The atheist must by virtual definition be an absolute villain, and to portray D'Amville's villainy Tourneur drew upon the by his time well-established tradition of the stage 'Machiavel',[1] itself derived, as I have elsewhere indicated, from a fusion of the Senecan villain-hero and the morality play Vice with popular misconceptions about the writings of Machiavelli.[2] Like such earlier 'Machiavels' as Kyd's Lorenzo, Marlowe's Barabas, and Shakespeare's Richard III, D'Amville derives a gleeful satisfaction from the contemplation of his own crimes, prides himself on his masterful command of 'policy', and when he is not with his confidant, Borachio, wears always the mask of a seeming virtue. His rational self-analysis and his justification of his evil deeds in intel-

---

stoics ruled the universe, Christians had only to substitute the providence of God, of which the laws of nature were a reflection. See Robert Hoopes, *Right Reason in the English Renaissance* (Cambridge, Mass., 1962).

[1] Cf. C. V. Boyer, *The Villain as Hero in Elizabethan Tragedy* (London, 1914), pp. 167–8.

[2] 'The Significance of Gentillet's *Contre-Machiavel*', *M.L.Q.*, X (1949), 153–7; 'Marlowe and Machiavelli', *Comparative Literature*, VI (1954), 349–56. Cf. also Mario Praz, 'The Politic Brain: Machiavelli and the Elizabethans', in *The Flaming Heart* (New York, 1958), pp. 90–145.

lectual terms carries on the tradition of the Senecan villain-hero in
particular.

Atheists were, as Ornstein points out,[1] generally regarded as
sensualists, 'atheist' and 'epicure' being virtually synonymous
terms, and the atheist being often defined as one who would evade
his duty to God out of a delusion which causes him to serve more
difficult masters, his own senses and the illusion of vainglory.
D'Amville thus can know no restriction on the gratification of his
own appetite.[2] The goal of man on earth he sees not as salvation,
but only as pleasure, profit, and power. D'Amville's philosophy is
made clear in the opening scene of the play in his conversation with
Borachio. It begins with an equation of man with beast, for to deny
God is implicitly to deny also that spiritual quality which man
derives from heaven and which separates him from the lower animals. If man differs in any way from the brute beasts, he holds, it
must be not because of God, but because of the special favour of
nature:

> Only a man's beholding to his Nature
> For th' better composition o' the two.
>
> (I. i. 8–9)

The human animal, living in accord with the law of nature and
knowing no superior power, is a self-sufficient entity who must
spend his time on earth in pursuit of pleasure and profit and who
must guide his conduct by his own rational powers. D'Amville even
deludes himself into believing that the man of reason can escape the
final fact of human mortality, that through his children he can live
for ever and thus retain the wealth which has been the sole mark of
his felicity, and to whose pursuit his life has been devoted. In this
expectation the audience sees already the extent of the atheist's delusion, for he has placed his hope in sons whose mortality is as
certain as his own. Marlowe's Tamburlaine, in a somewhat similar

---

[1] S.P., LI (1954), 198.

[2] That the 'reason' which has led D'Amville to this view is not 'right
reason' as Elizabethans conceived of it, is made clear by Thomas Wright,
The Passions of the minde (1594) [Sig. B5ʳ], where in differentiating between
reason and the passions he writes, 'for right reason oftentimes deprived
sense of those pleasures he had of long time enioyed'. Reason led not to
indulgence, but rather to abstinence.

manner, had trusted in his physical strength to shield him from the fact of human mortality, and Marlowe had shown the vanity of such aspiration. But Marlowe's superman does achieve all of which man is capable and is able at last to resign himself to the necessity of death, whereas what D'Amville achieves is finally revealed as nothing.

In its forthright didacticism the play carries on many features of the medieval *débat*. D'Amville proclaims his atheistical principles directly to the audience, both in soliloquies and in discussions with Borachio which show also the influence of the Senecan dialogue. Charlemont and Castabella proclaim in the same manner the virtues of Christian patience, chastity, and submission to divine will. By these beliefs they are preserved, whereas all of D'Amville's plots rebound upon himself. By ironic reversals we are reminded that as the atheist tries to destroy the virtuous he only succeeds in destroying himself. D'Amville and Borachio pride themselves always upon their cunning; they gloat over their machinations, so that the final disaster which overtakes them may demonstrate that their cunning has, in fact, been gross stupidity, and the 'reason' by which D'Amville has lived and which has led him to embrace his atheism has been only a self-deception and not true reason at all. He has relied upon what he calls 'the strength of natural understanding', but he learns at the end that

> Nature is a fool. There is a power
> Above her that hath overthrown the pride
> Of all my projects and posterity.
> (v. ii. 258-60)

One aspect of the play's debate between diabolic and heavenly values is in the conflict between chastity and lust which runs throughout, the one a traditional reflection of the perfect love of God, and the other an obvious symbol of the human animalism posited by a naturalist metaphysics. In a view of man as governed only by mechanical laws there may be a justification for animal sexuality as a reflection of these laws. Incest becomes defensible by analogy with the behaviour of the beasts, and in D'Amville's defence of this perversion he envies the lower animals who know no restriction in their pleasures:

> Incest, tush!
> These distances affinity observes
> Are articles of bondage cast upon
> Our freedoms by our own subjections.
> Nature allows a gen'ral liberty
> Of generation to all creatures else.
> Shall man, to whose command and use all creatures
> Were made subject, be less free than they?
>
> (IV. iii. 123–30)

To the naturalist who sees the force and power of nature as expressing themselves most fully in animal sexuality, moral law becomes
an unnatural restraint upon the laws of nature. To this argument
Castabella offers the answer of the play:

> O God,
> Is thy unlimited and infinite
> Omnipotence less free because thou dost
> No ill? Or if you argue merely out
> Of Nature, do you not degenerate
> From that, and are you not unworthy the
> Prerogative of Nature's masterpiece,
> When basely you prescribe yourself
> Authority and law from their examples
> Whom you should command?
>
> (IV. iii. 131–40)

This theme is reflected also in the opposition between Castabella
and Levidulcia. For Castabella, as her name implies, love is the
highest kind of chaste spiritual relationship:

> O love, thou chaste affection of the soul,
> Without th' adult'rate mixture of the blood,
> That virtue which to goodness addeth good,
> The minion of heaven's heart.
>
> (II. iii. 1–4)

Since Levidulcia, like D'Amville, denies the difference between
man and beast, love to her is lust or brute animal passion. Sharing
D'Amville's philosophy, moreover, she can only view this passion
as prescribed by the immutable laws of nature, and herself as a help-
less pawn subject to these laws:

> My strange affection to this man! 'Tis like
> That natural sympathy which e'en among

> The senseless creatures of the earth commands
> A mutual inclination and consent.
> For though it seems to be the free effect
> Of mine own voluntary love, yet I
> Can neither restrain it, nor give reason for 't.
>   (IV. v. 16–22)

This is the same fatalistic view of life which D'Amville in another context expresses:

> And I am of a confident belief
> That ev'n the time, place, manner of our deaths
> Do follow fate with that necessity
> That makes us sure to die. And in a thing
> Ordain'd so certainly unalterable,
> What can the use of providence prevail?
>   (I. ii. 46–51)

Animalism, mechanism, and determinism are all inseparably interwoven as facets of the atheism the play is designed to refute.

The involvement of Levidulcia with Fresco in a comic incident (II. v) based upon a well-known anecdote widely used in *novella* and *fabliau*[1] to render illicit love sordid and ridiculous is thus not to be regarded as mere comic relief by which Tourneur varies the serious didacticism of his main plot. The incident is designed as comic commentary upon the main plot, the animalism of Levidulcia being refuted by the satiric weapon of ridicule, just as that of D'Amville is to be refuted by the example of Charlemont and Castabella. The final punishment of Levidulcia parallels that of D'Amville in showing God's retribution for sin, and her dying repentance prepares the audience for that of D'Amville. In the same manner, the comedy of Languebeau Snuffe's attempted seduction of Soquette serves as commentary upon D'Amville's attempted rape of Castabella, with Charlemont as the instrument of divine providence who frustrates both evil-doers.

To make clear the central conflict of his play, Tourneur employs two conventional symbols, thunder and the stars,[2] each commonly used in literature as a sign of the divine presence in the universe. When D'Amville is counterfeiting grief at the death of Montferrers,

[1] See above, pp. xxx–xxxii.
[2] See J. M. S. Tompkins, 'Tourneur and the Stars', *R.E.S.*, XXII (1946), 315–19.

he expresses for the audience an orthodox Christian view of planet-
ary influence:

> Not one poor spark in the whole spacious sky
> Of all that endless number would vouchsafe
> To shine ? You viceroys to the king of Nature!
> Whose constellations govern mortal births,
> Where is that fatal planet rul'd at his
> Nativity ?   (II. iv. 34–9)

When he is alone with Borachio some lines later, however, he presents the contrary sceptical view, treating with scorn and derision
the notion that the stars, as reflections of the will of a power beyond
them, may exert influence upon human affairs:

> That power of rule philosophers ascribe
> To him they call the supreme of the stars,
> Making their influences governors
> Of sublunary creatures, when their selves
> Are senseless of their operations—
>   (II. iv. 136–40)

Although the denial of stellar influence was not uncommon among
the more enlightened of Tourneur's contemporaries, D'Amville
here is denying the existence of God, and at this very moment a
stage direction calls for '*Thunder and lightning*' as powerful evidence
that He whom the atheist mocks as merely called 'supreme of the
stars' does exist and will make His power felt.

To this striking evidence of divine presence D'Amville again
offers a counter-argument consonant with his naturalist philosophy, a pseudo-scientific explanation of thunder drawn from various
contemporary treatises:

> Dost start at thunder ? Credit my belief,
> 'Tis a mere effect of Nature,
> An exhalation hot and dry, involv'd
> Within a wat'ry vapour i' the middle
> Region of the air, whose coldness
> Congealing that thick moisture to a cloud,
> The angry exhalation shut within
> A prison of contrary quality,
> Strives to be free, and with the violent
> Eruption through the grossness of that cloud
> Makes this noise we hear.
>   (II. iv. 141–51)

It may be significant that when Charlemont is informed of the troubles at home through supernatural intervention in the form of his father's ghost appearing to him in a dream, and heralded also by '*Thunder and lightning*' to relate it to the supernatural phenomenon the audience has just beheld, he too at first reacts with a similar pseudo-scientific explanation of dreams (II. vi. 45–62), but he is soon convinced of the reality of his supernatural warning:

> O pardon me. My doubtful heart was slow
> To credit that which I did fear to know.
>   (II. vi. 68–9)

The thunder and lightning motif appears again when D'Amville is about to ravish Castabella, and she calls for divine intervention:

> O patient Heav'n, why dost thou not express
> Thy wrath in thunderbolts, to tear the frame
> Of man in pieces ? How can earth endure
> The burden of this wickedness without
> An earthquake, or the angry face of Heav'n
> Be not enflam'd with lightning ?
>   (IV. iii. 162–7)

The power of heaven is made apparent by the immediate appearance of Charlemont, who frightens D'Amville away, showing again the intervention of God to protect the innocent.

When D'Amville in the churchyard begins 'to feel / The loathsome horror of my sin' (IV. iii. 223–4), he sees the stars as reminders of the divine retribution which awaits him:

> . . . she meets me
> I' the face with all her light corrupted eyes
> To challenge payment o' me.
>   (IV. iii. 227–9)

And he comes to see the thunder also as a symbol of divine power which must destroy him:

> O were my body circumvolv'd
> Within that cloud, that when the thunder tears
> His passage open, it might scatter me
> To nothing in the air!
>   (IV. iii. 248–51)

But at the beginning of the fifth act, in which the atheism of

D'Amville will be finally refuted, he again denies the power of the
stars and sees his gold instead as the source of all power:

> Behold, thou ignorant astronomer,
> Whose wand'ring speculation seeks among
> The planets for men's fortunes! With amazement
> Behold thine error and be planet-struck.
> These are the stars whose operations make
> The fortunes and the destinies of men.
> Yond' lesser eyes of Heav'n, like subjects rais'd
> Into their lofty houses when their prince
> Rides underneath th' ambition of their loves,
> Are mounted only to behold the face
> Of your most rich imperious eminence
> With unprevented sight.
>
> (v. i. 10–21)

This blasphemy, which would exalt worldly wealth above the
power of the stars, is immediately refuted. First the ghost of Montferrers enters to remind him that 'with all thy wisdom th' art a fool'
(v. i. 27). Then follow the deaths of his sons, whose cure all the
power of his gold cannot effect, to remind him of his own mortality.
Finally, when D'Amville is fully aware of the punishment which is
being visited upon him, the star motif appears again:

> Now to myself I am ridiculous.
> Nature, thou art a traitor to my soul.
> Thou hast abus'd my trust. I will complain
> To a superior court to right my wrong.
> I'll prove thee a forger of false assurances.
> In yond' Star Chamber thou shalt answer it.
>
> (v. i. 115–20)

The *double entendre* is very effective. In the high court of the stars
his relation to nature will be resolved.

Because he is an atheist the destruction of D'Amville is inevitable, but we must note that in spite of his damnation he is no longer
an atheist when he dies. His final recognition of the providence of
God is in accord with a widespread Renaissance belief that few men
died atheists, being converted usually by some extraordinary evidence of divine presence some time before their deaths.[1] D'Amville

---

[1] Cf. Martin Fotherby, *Atheomastix* (1622), p. 143: 'Yea, and even the
very Heathen themselves do insinuate, that the iustice of God so presseth

plays the traditional role of the dying sinner coming too late to
recognize the error of his ways, which recalls the deaths of Marlowe's Faustus and Shakespeare's Richard III and Macbeth.

We note a wavering of D'Amville's confidence in nature as soon
as his plans begin to backfire; he begins gradually to question his
once strongly held beliefs until at the end he is ready to renounce
them entirely. There is a gross macabre humour in the graveyard
scenes which mark the beginning of this conversion. D'Amville is
terrified by the signs of death, and he is able to contrast his own
fears with Charlemont's brave acceptance of mortality. The atheist's realization of his own weakness in this respect—atheists were
all cowards according to Renaissance moralists—causes him to
doubt the validity of his own creed. When he sees Charlemont and
Castabella sleeping peacefully upon their death's head pillows, he
has a vision of a kind of felicity to which his own 'reason' has been
incapable of leading him:

> Stay. Asleep ? So soundly ? And so sweetly upon death's heads ?
> And in a place so full of fear and horror ? Sure there is some other
> happiness within the freedom of the conscience than my know-
> ledge e'er attained to.
>
> (IV. iii. 284–7)

Seeing his own hope of immortality finally destroyed by the deaths
of his two sons, D'Amville is forced to conclude that this disaster
cannot be accounted for in terms of the mechanistic impersonal
nature in which he has believed, and for the first time he acknow-
ledges a supernatural power:

> Can Nature be
> So simple or malicious to destroy
> The reputation of her proper memory ?
> She cannot. Sure there is some power above
> Her that controls her force.
>
> (V. i. 100–4)

---

the Atheists (though they be his most hardned, and confirmed enemies)
that it not onely inforceth them to confesse him upon earth; but also to
proclaime him out of Hell it selfe. And from thence to confesse, both their
owne sinne and wickednesse, and Gods most iust vengeance: exhorting
others to take heede by their examples.' Cited by Ornstein, *S.P.*, LI (1954),
202.

Ornstein has argued, rather ingeniously,[1] that D'Amville's view of nature is never really refuted in the play, that his conversion involves merely a rejection of nature in favour of moral law, and that Tourneur therefore accepts a dichotomy between the two which looks forward to Bacon and Hobbes. Elizabethan moralists, of course, could allow for no such separation. In the doctor's answer to D'Amville there is all the rejection of the atheist position the play requires, for the doctor is saying that nature is the creation of God, ruled by God, and thus axiomatically it must reflect divine will, which is synonymous with moral law:

> A power above Nature?
> Doubt you that, my lord? Consider but
> Whence man receives his body and his form:
> Not from corruption like some worms and flies,
> But only from the generation of
> A man, for Nature never did bring forth
> A man without a man; nor could the first
> Man, being but the passive subject, not
> The active mover, be the maker of
> Himself; so of necessity there must
> Be a superior power to Nature.
>   (v. i. 104–14)

The entire play is shaped as a rejection of D'Amville's position, as is clear also from the constant dwelling on the motif of 'reason'. D'Amville's view of nature has been faulty from the first because it has resulted from a 'reason' which was not the 'right reason' of Renaissance moralists in that it was not guided by divine grace and thus could never reflect more than the subjection to sin of a fallen mankind.[2] It was axiomatic that man could never arrive at truth by the power of his own mind alone, for human reason had been clouded by original sin.

In the court scene with which the play ends, reminiscent of such scenes at the endings of Jonson's comedies, there is a reaffirmation of order. The shallowness of D'Amville's position is exposed by the superior ability of Charlemont and Castabella to face death bravely, and their joyful rescue is offered as evidence of the heavenly power

---

[1] S.P., LI (1954), 206–7; The Moral Vision, pp. 126–7.
[2] See Hoopes, op. cit., passim.

which the atheist had denied. Cataplasma, Soquette, and Fresco
receive the punishment which in a just moral order must be visited
upon the wicked, and the Puritan whose religious hypocrisy D'Amville had used as an argument against all religion (I. ii. 210–15) is
unmasked as Snuffe, the tallow-chandler, and sent on his way. Then
the judge is ready to 'resolve you of your question' (v. ii. 96), which
is in essence the question of the play, to teach D'Amville just what
it is which enables Charlemont to face death without fear. The
atheist must now 'find out / Th' efficient cause of a contented
mind' (v. ii. 166–7).

Charlemont and Castabella can die bravely because they have
their virtue to sustain them:

> Our lives cut off
> In our young prime of years are like green herbs
> Wherewith we strew the hearses of our friends,
> For as their virtue gather'd when th' are green,
> Before they wither or corrupt, is best,
> So we in virtue are the best for death
> While yet we have not liv'd to such an age
> That the increasing canker of our sins
> Hath spread too far upon us.
>   (v. ii. 132–40)

Castabella in these lines is welcoming death as a means of escape
from that involvement in sin which Tourneur saw as inherent in
the human condition. To die young is to die with the maximum of
virtue, and such virtue is itself a greater good than life, for through
it man may attain heaven, the good that is permanent and real.
These chaste lovers can die bravely because of that contempt for
the world which was so basic to medieval Christianity, and which
made necessary the life of virtue which might lead to heaven. There
is a paradox here, for the virtue arising out of scorn for worldly
things itself makes life on earth more beautiful. Thus the earthly
felicity which D'Amville has sought in a contrary manner comes
instead to Charlemont and Castabella who have put their hopes
only in heaven. Castabella and Charlemont in their welcoming of
death reveal to the atheist the final worthlessness of the worldly
pleasure, wealth, and power which have been the goals of his existence.

D

D'Amville receives a further answer to his question with the very blow which strikes out his own brains, for this miraculous accident gives evidence of the divine intervention in human affairs in which Charlemont and Castabella have placed their faith. It is fitting that D'Amville should be struck in the very seat of his perverted 'reason'. In the justice of his own death, D'Amville recognizes the power of a righteous providence:

> but yond' power that struck me knew
> The judgment I deserv'd, and gave it.
>   (v. ii. 265–6)

Again the point is emphasized for the audience by the judge as he points to the new felicity of Charlemont and Castabella:

> Strange is his death and judgment. With the hands
> Of joy and justice I thus set you free.
> The power of that eternal providence
> Which overthrew his projects in their pride
> Hath made your griefs the instruments to raise
> Your blessings to a greater height than ever.
>   (v. ii. 269–74)

Out of man's very ability to scorn the evanescent things of this world and to suffer the world's evil with Christian patience must emerge his final blessings, and it is significant that the consistent virtue of Charlemont and Castabella assures them of happiness not only in heaven but in the present world as well. In Tourneur's use of the medieval philosophy of *contemptus mundi* there is a basis not only for attaining heaven but for living the moral life on earth.

The tragic progression of D'Amville receives the principal emphasis of the play. It is inseparable, however, from the parallel complex of events in which Charlemont is involved, and these events are related to the tradition of revenge tragedy which by Tourneur's time had been well established upon the English stage.[1] But Charlemont is a strange kind of revenge play hero, not because of an unusual ethic on the part of the author, but because Charlemont exemplifies the kind of action of which most revenge play heroes were incapable.

---

[1] See F. T. Bowers, *Elizabethan Revenge Tragedy 1587–1642* (Princeton, 1940); Percy Simpson, 'The Theme of Revenge in Elizabethan Tragedy', in *Studies in Elizabethan Drama* (Oxford, 1955), pp. 138–78.

Seneca's own tragedy of revenge, of which we may take his
Thyestes as perhaps the best example, was itself intensely moral,
emphasizing always the fact of *nemesis*, with blood calling for blood,
and the criminal always suffering punishment, not only in his own
person, but in his descendants as well. It is sometimes forgotten
that most Elizabethan revenge tragedies, as Bowers makes clear,
are moral as well. While audiences may have delighted above all in
the sensationalism and spectacle of horror, the heroes of such plays
—Chettle's *Hoffman* provides an excellent example—tended to
vitiate themselves by the very act of vengeance-seeking and to die
as fully tainted by evil as the villains who had injured them. Bowers
is probably right in finding this to be true of Kyd's Hieronimo in
The Spanish Tragedy, although there is considerable ambivalence
in this play, as in Marston's *Antonio's Revenge*. Sympathy for blood
revenge as a debt of honour, in spite of the Christian injunction, is
so deeply rooted in European folk tradition that even Dante, the
most Christian of poets, could write 'Che bell'onor s'acquista in
far vendetta' (*Canzone*, XII, 83), and in his *Divine Comedy* (*Inferno*,
XXIX, 31-5) dwell with sympathy upon the shame inherent in failure
to avenge the murder of a kinsman. But even those critics who have
held that Hieronimo escapes the degeneration of a Hoffman have
so argued on the assumption that his official position as a magistrate
charged with the execution of justice permits him the right of vengeance, and they have suggested that Kyd cast his play to reveal
Hieronimo as an agent of God executing divine purpose,[1] although
it is difficult to reconcile his murder of Castile with his role either
as magistrate or as divine instrument. The greater revenge plays of
the age involve a tension between the contrary demands of divine
law and retribution as a debt of honour, and there is a strong emotional commitment to the cause of the avenger. *The Atheist's Tragedy*, like Chapman's *Revenge of Bussy D'Ambois*, stands apart from
such plays in offering us a hero who refuses to revenge. In opposition to the call of blood for blood, Chapman's Clermont asserts a

---

[1] Cf. Philip Edwards, ed., *The Spanish Tragedy* (London, 1959),
pp. l–lxi; S. F. Johnson, '*The Spanish Tragedy*, or Babylon Revisited', in
Essays on Shakespeare and Elizabethan Drama in Honor of Hardin Craig
(Columbia, Mo., 1962), pp. 23–36.

classical stoicism, while Tourneur's Charlemont asserts the Christian patience preached by Tudor moralists.

We must remember that, in spite of the sympathy for the avenger which appears often in Elizabethan drama, Tourneur's age was one in which the taking of private revenge was condemned as morally wrong, a sin directly against God who had reserved the punishment of sinners as his own prerogative.[1] An awareness of this ethical conviction is crucial to an understanding of both of Tourneur's plays. It is basic to *The Revenger's Tragedy*, where Vindice is destroyed by his own pursuit of vengeance and where the contrasting Antonio, who has suffered injuries parallel to those of Vindice, by his Christian patience and refusal to avenge his wrongs attains the final triumph.[2]

There were two facets of the theory of revenge as promulgated by Tudor moralists. Not only was private revenge forbidden, but heavenly vengeance upon evil-doers was considered inevitable. There was thus a prohibition of present action combined with a promise of future action. Miss Campbell cites Pierre de la Primaudaye's *The French Academy*,[3] that great compendium of Renaissance moral philosophy, as illustration of both these principles:

> Therefore wee may well conclude, that all priuate Revenge proceeding of envy, or of hatred, or of anger, is vicious and forbidden by God, who commaundeth us to render good for evill, and not evill for evill. . . And as himselfe commeth in judgement to take vengeance, so hee woulde have them that supplie his place among men [i.e., kings and magistrates], unto whome hee hath committed the sworde for the defence of the good and punishment of evill doers, to followe his example. But whether they doe so or no, there is no sinne that can avoide punishment, and that findeth not a

[1] This has been well demonstrated by L. B. Campbell, 'Theories of Revenge in Renaissance England', *M.P.*, xxviii (1930–1), 281–96.

[2] 'God's revenge', as Miss Campbell writes (p. 293), 'is the general theme dominating all the tragedies of the period; the revenge play is concerned with one variant of this theme, that of private revenge in relation to God's revenge.' This important fact was generally ignored by such early writers on revenge tragedy as E. E. Stoll, *John Webster*, pp. 94–152, and A. H. Thorndike, 'The Relations of *Hamlet* to Contemporary Revenge Plays', *P.M.L.A.*, xvii (1902), 125–220.

[3] Tr. by T. B. (Thomas Bowes) (1594), pp. 326–7.

Judge even in him that committed it, to take vengeance thereof by meanes of the affections, which God hath placed in man to that end.

The vengeance of God inevitably will be executed, even by the sinner upon himself should there be no other means. We need not assume that this was a doctrine to which all Elizabethans assented; the very need of Tudor moralists constantly to assert it may suggest that many theatre-goers could sympathize with the blood revenger. But Tourneur's play is a didactic work designed to assert the orthodox position as clearly as it is asserted by de la Primaudaye.

In *The Revenger's Tragedy* Tourneur had mirrored the two facets of this doctrine of revenge in Vindice and Antonio, although the emphasis of the play had been upon Vindice, with the behaviour of Antonio to place that of the hero in perspective. In *The Atheist's Tragedy* Charlemont fulfils a similar role in relation to D'Amville, about whom the principal action centres. Charlemont is everything which the atheist is not. He sees man as a creature of spirit, controlled by a just and omnipotent deity to whom he is always subject. His 'reason' is the recognition of divine law which leads him to a mastery of his own passions, so that he is always the 'Senecal man'[1] who can never be vanquished by the blows of fortune:

> But now I am an emp'ror of a world,
> This little world of man. My passions are
> My subjects, and I can command them laugh,
> Whilst thou dost tickle 'em to death with misery.
>   (III. iii. 44–7)

His universe is a divinely ordered one, where the sufferings of mankind are always in just proportion to their sins:

> I grant thee, Heaven, thy goodness doth command
> Our punishments, but yet no further than
> The measure of our sins. How should they else
> Be just ? Or how should that good purpose of
> Thy justice take effect by bounding men
> Within the confines of humanity,
> When our afflictions do exceed our crimes ?
>   (III. iii. 1–7)

He is, in short, a model of Christian patience who submits freely to

---

[1] Cf. Michael Higgins, 'The Development of the Senecal Man', *R.E.S.*, XXIII (1947), 24–33.

the pain and misery of life, confident always of the perfection and
justice of God's plan, ready to accept whatever misfortune comes
his way in the assurance that good must at last triumph. He reflects
the attitude towards life which moralists like Guillaume du Vair[1]
preached:

> It is indeed the greatest, and surest comfort man can receiue, and
> take in publike, and priuate calamities, to perswade himselfe, that
> whatsoeuer befalleth him is ordained by that eternall power, dis-
> tributed by that infinite wisedome, which gouerneth the world
> with the same goodnesse and Iustice wherewithall he created it.
> When this opinion is once rooted in the heart of man, I doe not
> see what windes can shake his constancie.

Charlemont's eyes are fixed steadily upon heaven, which he even
thanks for his misfortunes when out of them he sees his final happiness emerging:

> For all my wrongs I thank thee, gracious Heav'n;
> Th' hast made me satisfaction, to reserve
> Me for this blessed purpose.
>   (IV. iii. 178–80)

He is always ready for death, since heaven represents the only permanent value to which man can aspire. He sees as folly:

> That man with so much labour should aspire
> To worldly height, when in the humble earth
> The world's condition's at the best! Or scorn
> Inferior men, since to be lower than
> A worm is to be higher than a king.
>   (IV. iii. 18–22)

Charlemont expresses his Christian patience most markedly in
his role as a revenge play hero. Like other such heroes, he is visited
by a ghost, but this ghost counsels not vengeance but Christian
submission:

> Attend with patience the success of things,
> But leave revenge unto the King of kings.
>   (II. vi. 22–3)

And when Charlemont has momentarily forgotten his father's
counsel and has stabbed Sebastian in a fit of passion, his father's
ghost appears again to warn him:

[1] *Op. cit.* [Sig. I4ʳ].

> Hold, Charlemont!
> Let him revenge my murder and thy wrongs
> To whom the justice of revenge belongs.
>   (III. ii. 32–4)

The parallel with Shakespeare's *Hamlet* here is close, for Hamlet too sees his father's ghost appear to guide him when, in his mother's closet, he seems, although in a different context from that of Tourneur's play, to be varying from a proper course of action. Charlemont, like Hamlet, is tortured 'between the passion of / My blood and the religion of my soul' (III. ii. 35–6), but he nevertheless accepts his father's injunction, allows his reason to overcome his passion, and never varies from the true Christian path. He never seeks to raise his hand against his persecutor, and he patiently places his head upon the block, unafraid to die because his faith in heavenly justice has never wavered. When heaven acts at last and intervenes to spare his life, he speaks the moral for the audience:

> Only to Heav'n I attribute the work,
> Whose gracious motives made me still forbear
> To be mine own revenger. Now I see
> That *patience is the honest man's revenge*.
>   (v. ii. 275–8)

The Atheist's Tragedy is a new kind of revenge play in that the revenger is victorious through refusal to revenge, rather than destroyed, like Vindice, for the vehemence of his vengeance. In its ethical viewpoint it may not differ so markedly from *Hamlet* as some critics have supposed, for it is possible to argue, although not all readers will agree, that Shakespeare's hero murders Claudius at last not as a private avenger, but as God's agent administering public justice,[1] and in his death there is a large measure of victory. In Tourneur's play there is little of the tragic conflict or tension between opposing systems of value which makes Shakespeare's so infinitely greater, but Charlemont is Tourneur's own way of answering the question of how a good man may live in a world corrupted by the reality of sin and death, and it is an answer in terms of a traditional Christianity.

[1] Cf. Fredson Bowers, 'Hamlet as Scourge and Minister', *P.M.L.A.*, LXX (1955), 740–9.

There is far more to *The Atheist's Tragedy*, however, than its doctrinal argument; indeed this argument is so simple and commonplace that the play could have little interest for a modern reader were this its principal value. *The Atheist's Tragedy* is, in fact, a work of tremendous variety, probably unique in its age for its manner of combining seemingly incongruous elements. It is rich in comedy of different kinds. The preoccupation with death and sexuality, combined with the most ludicrous of situations, gives to the graveyard scene (IV. iii) a gothic quality we encounter in no other play. Misadventures in darkness occur often in Elizabethan drama, as, for instance, in *The Merry Devil of Edmonton*, but nowhere are they given the effect of *Walpurgisnacht* which we find in Tourneur's play.

Much of the humour is based upon word-play, often very clever, almost always obscene, with a skilful evocation of traditional sexual symbols. The description of Soquette's tapestry (IV. i) is a virtual lesson in Renaissance iconography. This under-language of comic sexuality seems at times to be a comment upon the chastity of Charlemont and Castabella—itself rigid almost to the point of absurdity—so that it may appear as if the dramatist, perhaps in spite of himself, is growing fascinated as the play progresses with the very sexuality he is seeking to reject. This comedy of *double entendre* conditions the tone of *The Atheist's Tragedy*, just as the situation-comedy involving Fresco and Snuffe, also sexual, is used, as I have indicated, to underscore the central moral themes of the play by comic commentary. The anti-Puritan satire, centred in Languebeau Snuffe, reflects also upon the moral pretensions of the virtuous characters. The skill with which this satire is handled is equalled perhaps by few writers other than Marston, whose example Tourneur may well have had in mind. *The Atheist's Tragedy* might have been a dull and insipid morality play, but it is rescued from this fate by the extraordinary (if somewhat macabre) sense of humour which is one of Tourneur's surest qualities.

There is also in this play, so full of ludicrous and impossible incident, a strange quality of realism, a feeling of familiar domesticity which helps us to accept events which otherwise we might reject as incredible. The home life of D'Amville and his family is presented with an unusual intimacy which causes us to feel at home in the world of the play, and in the household of Cataplasma we are given an insight into an area of Jacobean life such as we can find in few places other than in the Bellafront scenes of Dekker's *Honest Whore*. Much of our sympathy for D'Amville may be engendered by this quality of intimacy as we are taken into his confidence and participate in the easy fellowship of his household. There is even in the portrait of D'Amville a certain amount of psychological probing on Tourneur's part, for the atheist does not begin with incest. He comes to it at the last, after he has been driven from one resource to another to secure his somewhat pathetic ends.

Tourneur has a sure sense of the sensational and the theatrically effective. He couches his pietistic moral lesson in a rich assortment of thrilling episodes. We have a ghost, murders committed upon the stage, an elaborate and formal funeral ceremony, seduction and attempted rape, all the gothic panoply of graves and dead men's skulls, not one but two concealed lovers whose presence the deceived husband may at any moment discover, and all is capped with the death of the hero in a stage execution as bizarre and unusual as any performed upon the Jacobean stage. In the suicide of Levidulcia, overcome by the enormity of her sins, there is the kind of sentimental melodrama in which Jacobean audiences delighted.

We have also a great variety of place settings: ordinary Jacobean households, the darkened fields where murderers lurk, an army camp, a prison, the house of a bawd, and finally a court of justice. *The Atheist's Tragedy* offers as comprehensive and realistic a view of Jacobean daily life as any play of the period. Tourneur knew how to give his audience all that it wanted, and yet none of the diverse elements of his play seems out of place, for all contribute to a remarkable unity of tone, constituting a dramatic world, at once real and unreal, which is always credible.

c. Imagery
The Revenger's Tragedy is the greater of Tourneur's artistic achievements because it is able to translate a moral vision into emotional terms in a manner which *The Atheist's Tragedy* does not attempt. This difference between the two plays is reflected in their poetry,

that of the earlier play being characterized by rapid movement and
passionate intensity,[1] that of the later and more intellectual work
by a slowness and precision, a clarity of statement to be expected in
a drama of exposition and logical argument. The language of *The
Atheist's Tragedy*, as Jenkins has written,[2] is

> the nearest we get before Massinger to that masterly lucidity of
> exposition which is one of Massinger's principal merits in dramatic
> poetry, though it often at the same time brings his verse down to
> the lower key of prose. In Tourneur it arises because the emotion
> is for the time being overlaid with serious thought.

The poetry of *The Atheist's Tragedy* is, in short, a different kind of
poetry from that of the earlier play, less powerful because it attempts to do different things, but of an excellence uniquely its own.

Such poetry demands a kind of imagery whose function is not
immediate emotional impact and revelation, but what Miss Eke-
blad[3] has called 'clarifying amplification'. By illustration and ela-
boration imagery furthers the play's logical argument. In this respect, the building imagery, whose dominance in the play M. C.
Bradbrook also has noted,[4] is closely integrated with the play's
structure and moral argument, the various instances in which it
occurs being carefully linked as parts of a logical progression. When
the first step in D'Amville's plan has been taken, the false report of
Charlemont's death, this is established as the foundation of the
house by which the atheist's fortunes will be symbolized:

> So. The foundation's laid. Now by degrees
> The work will rise and soon be perfected.
>
> (II. i. 122–3)

The future tense looks forward to the murder itself, which will represent the first stones of the house, as Borachio suggests as he is
about to commit the crime:

---

[1] 'His phrases', writes T. S. Eliot, *Selected Essays*, p. 191, 'seem to contract the images in his effort to say everything in the least space, the shortest
time.'

[2] *R.E.S.*, XVII (1941), 25.

[3] 'An Approach to Tourneur's Imagery', *M.L.R.*, LIV (1959), 489–98.

[4] *Themes and Conventions of Elizabethan Tragedy* (Cambridge, 1935),
pp. 175–6.

> Such stones men use to raise a house upon,
> But with these stones I go to ruin one.
>
> (II. iv. 1–2)

When the murder has been accomplished we are reminded by the reappearance of the same poetic image that D'Amville's monstrous plans are well under way. Of the place where the dead man's head was laid he says

> Upon this ground I'll build my manor house,
> And this shall be the chiefest corner-stone.
>
> (II. iv. 99–100)

The tenses have moved from the future of anticipation to the present of accomplishment to anticipation of further development, and they foreshadow the pluperfect tense with which D'Amville will again use building imagery in lamenting the ruin of his fortunes, which is the collapse of the house begun with the initial report of Charlemont's supposed death:

> There is a power
> Above her that hath overthrown the pride
> Of all my projects and posterity,
> For whose surviving blood I had erected
> A proud monument.
>
> (v. ii. 258–62)

By iterative imagery Tourneur has stressed the successive stages in D'Amville's career and given poetic expression to the moral statement implicit in the atheist's destruction.

Miss Ekeblad (p. 492) calls attention to the skilful manner in which Tourneur uses this same class of imagery for ironic comment, irony being one of the principal means by which the moral substance of the play is made clear. At the beginning of the fifth act D'Amville uses a building image to congratulate himself on the success of his machinations:

> My real wisdom has rais'd up a state
> That shall eternize my posterity.
>
> (v. i. 46–7)

But when D'Amville has seen his hopes of immortality collapse with the death of his sons, he returns to the same poetic image, using it now with a new significance:

His gasping sighs are like the falling noise
Of some great building when the groundwork breaks.
On these two pillars stood the stately frame
And architecture of my lofty house.
An earthquake shakes 'em; the foundation shrinks.

(v. i. 75–9)

Although individual images in *The Atheist's Tragedy* are sometimes very complex, we are not struck by a random piling of image upon image, with a rich profusion of sensory impressions. There is, rather, a logical movement from image to image in which each succeeds the former in a proper order. This appears in such sustained rhetorical speeches as Charlemont's farewell to Castabella (I. ii. 68–87), Levidulcia's urging her daughter to marry (I. iv. 79–101), the description of the siege of Ostend (II. i. 40–94), and elsewhere throughout the play. This use of imagery as an instrument of exposition and argument is a striking feature of *The Atheist's Tragedy*, not to be found to the same extent in many other plays of the era.

Professor Ellis-Fermor has divided the imagery of the play into four large categories.[1] These include not only that drawn from building, but also imagery based upon 'kingship and the apparatus of government', upon 'business and financial transactions', and upon 'outdoor nature in the specialized form of water and river imagery'. These are all conventional categories which may be found in the work of other dramatists. What is remarkable is the manner in which Tourneur uses them. Another such distinctive characteristic of Tourneur's imagery has been noticed by Elizabeth Holmes.[2] This is a certain metaphysical quality, a richness of word-play, with a blending of pun and image, so that metaphors are extended and developed through the exploration of the associations and secondary meanings of words.

The commercial imagery which Professor Ellis-Fermor has noted is used to emphasize the crassness of worldly values, and Tourneur's word-play technique appears notably in the passage with which Charlemont accepts the supposed friendship of Languebeau Snuffe:

[1] *M.L.R.*, xxx (1935), 289–301.
[2] *Aspects of Elizabethan Imagery* (Oxford, 1929), pp. 109–16.

> Sir, I will take your friendship up at use.
> And fear not that your profit shall be small;
> Your interest shall exceed your principal.
>
> (I. ii. 146–8)

Here the simple 'take up', meaning 'to accept', by the addition of
'at use' (interest), is given a commercial implication so that it means
'to borrow', and the accepting of friendship becomes the borrowing
of money at interest. Then the succession of commercial terms,
'profit', 'interest', 'principal', underscores poetically for the audience the sordid basis of what Charlemont is accepting as genuine
friendship.

A similar technique is used in the speech of D'Amville which
closes the scene of his murder of Montferrers:

> Now farewell black night,
> Thou beauteous mistress of a murderer;
> To honour thee, that hast accomplish'd all,
> I'll wear thy colours at his funeral.
>
> (II. iv. 178–81)

Here the personification of 'night' as a mistress leads by natural
association to the favour such a mistress might grant her lover to
wear in her honour, and this becomes a cloth of black, the traditional symbol of death (conventionally equated with night), which
D'Amville will wear at Charlemont's funeral, the place of his
triumph and murder's consummation.

The star motif which, as we have seen, has been dominant
throughout the play, culminates in the final act in the same kind
of word-play (v. i. 117–20), and the metaphysical exploration of the
limits of a metaphor appears notably in Levidulcia's death speech,
reminiscent of John Donne's *A Valediction, Of Weeping*, in its playing upon the tear motif:

> But what can tears do good?
> When I weep only water, they weep blood.
> But could I make an ocean with my tears,
> That on the flood this broken vessel of
> My body, laden heavy with light lust,
> Might suffer shipwreck and so drown my shame,
> Then weeping were to purpose.
>
> (IV. v. 71–7)

Tears become an ocean, and by association her body the vessel to
float upon it. The alliteration and antithesis reinforce the double
meanings in 'laden heavy with light lust' ('heavy' also meaning
'sad', and 'light' also meaning 'wanton'), and in the drowning of
her body in tears the metaphor is completed, with repetition of
'weeping' in the final line to bring us back to the point at which it
began.

When D'Amville is suffering his pangs of terror in the churchyard, night, who at II. iv. 178–81 had been his mistress, is now the
bawd who has catered to his lust, the world a brothel, and murder
the strumpet with whom he has sinned:

> And that bawd,
> The sky there, she could shut the windows and
> The doors of this great chamber of the world,
> And draw the curtains of the clouds between
> Those lights and me about this bed of earth,
> When that same strumpet, Murder, and myself
> Committed sin together. Then she could
> Leave us i' the dark till the close deed
> Was done.
>
> (IV. iii. 215–23)

These lines, which Professor Ellis-Fermor (p. 300) has called 'the
passage which represents the culminating achievement of imagery
in either play', are marked by the same metaphysical, yet logical and
coherent, technique, each metaphor giving way by association to
the next and the consistency of every image maintained throughout. This is poetry of a kind beyond the range of anything in *The
Revenger's Tragedy*, whose lesser maturity of style is by contrast at
once apparent. It is not often, unfortunately, that Tourneur is able
to maintain this poetic level in *The Atheist's Tragedy*.

d. *Tourneur, Chapman, Marlowe, and Shakespeare*

It is very likely that, as has been suggested,[1] Tourneur was moved
in writing *The Atheist's Tragedy* by a need to reply to Chapman's
Bussy plays. D'Amville may be Tourneur's attempt to place his
own view of the moral implications of Chapman's Bussy into clear

[1] Cf. above, pp. xxiv–xxv.

perspective, as the Christian patience of his Charlemont may have
been framed in opposition to the classical stoicism of Clermont
D'Ambois. The animalistic passion of Levidulcia is almost a parody
of the force which drives Chapman's Tamyra to Bussy,[1] and the
Christian ghost of Montferrers may have been Tourneur's answer
to the ghosts of more questionable morality who appear in both of
Chapman's plays.

   In framing his tragedy of an apostate Tourneur may have drawn
also upon the example of Marlowe's *Doctor Faustus*, although *The
Atheist's Tragedy* lacks the power of Marlowe's tragedy—among
other reasons, because D'Amville does not have the heroic stature
of a Faustus, and because his rejection of God is merely an intellectual proposition, without the emotional commitment to a contrary
ideal which in itself has some validity and which may thus enable
an audience to share vicariously in the heroic aspirations of Faustus,
in the painful futility of their frustration, and in the horror of the
final price he must pay. *The Atheist's Tragedy* may well be offering
an answer to *Faustus* in its holding up of the felicity of Charlemont
and Castabella as an ideal against which the folly of D'Amville's
rejection of God may be measured, whereas in Marlowe's play, in
spite of a finer perception of Christianity, there is no such affirmation, only the horror of a view of damnation as the price of human
striving, and little indication that the Christian scheme which
Faustus rejects in his opening speech might have been a worth-
while alternative.

   In this sense of affirmation *The Atheist's Tragedy* is perhaps more
closely related to Shakespeare's tragedy of apostasy, *Macbeth*, and
the several echoes of this play, noted in the commentary, would
suggest that Tourneur was familiar with it as well. Compared with
Macbeth, D'Amville is too much of a caricature to reveal the imagination and the emotional grasp of his own infamy which enables us
to participate fully in the fall of Shakespeare's hero and to feel a
oneness with him in spite of the enormity of his crimes. It may be
argued, nevertheless, that in his confutation of Chapman the dramatist upon whom Tourneur drew most heavily for example was
William Shakespeare. This discipleship appears not only in Tour-

[1] See note at IV. v. 16–22.

neur's moral attitudes, but in his choice of situation and poetic
language as well.

That *The Atheist's Tragedy* bears a close resemblance to Shakespeare's *Hamlet* has been noted by many critics. Not only are passages and incidents of the earlier play echoed by Tourneur, but
both plays belong within the larger context of the revenge play tradition. It has been argued commonly[1] that Tourneur's is a kind of
answer to Shakespeare's play, in which he seeks to counter Shakespeare's 'theory of revenge' with a more Christian view. But that
Tourneur's conception of the morality of revenge is so opposed to
Shakespeare's as such writers as McGinn suppose is a notion which,
as I have suggested,[2] is open to serious question.

That Tourneur was among Shakespeare's most persistent imi-
tators may even more surely be observed in the relationship of *The
Atheist's Tragedy* to *King Lear*, which, as Levin L. Schucking appears to have been the first to argue in detail,[3] is a very close one.
The verbal echoes of *King Lear*, noted in the commentary, are very
numerous, but even more striking is the relation of D'Amville to
Shakespeare's Edmund, who espouses the same naturalistic philosophy and who undergoes the same kind of death-bed repentance
when the folly of his dependence upon a reason not guided by divine
grace has been revealed to him. The Christian patience of Charlemont is in the same way foreshadowed by that of Edgar. It has been
suggested also[4] that the distracted D'Amville calling for judgment
in the final act may owe something to the model of the mad King
Lear upon the heath.

It may well be that Tourneur's use of thunder and the stars to
accent poetically the meaning of his play, which, as has been noted,[5]
is a device of crucial importance in *The Atheist's Tragedy*, was suggested by Shakespeare's use of these same poetic symbols in *King
Lear*. Interpretations of Shakespeare's play differ widely, of course,

---

[1] See, for instance, D. J. McGinn, *Shakespeare's Influence on the Drama
of his Age* (New Brunswick, N.J., 1938), pp. 30–7.

[2] Cf. above, p. lv.

[3] 'Eine Anleihe Shakespeares bei Tourneur', *Englische Studien*, L (1916–
17), 80–103.

[4] Ornstein, *The Moral Vision of Jacobean Tragedy*, p. 121.

[5] Cf. above, pp. xliii–xlvi.

but most readers will recognize three main stages in Shakespeare's conception of Lear: the savage pride and blind self-assurance of the opening scenes, the madness and self-examination of the central scenes, and the calm resignation which follows Lear's reunion with Cordelia. The thunder motif is used by Shakespeare to accompany these three stages in his hero's progression. When first Lear hurries out into the storm, full only of his own sense of injury and outrage and unaware of his own role in his disaster, he sees thunder as a demonic force by which the gods may execute their vengeance upon mankind, and he calls for its manifestation, much as it is invoked by Castabella (IV. iii. 162–7) and D'Amville (IV. iii. 248–51) in Tourneur's play:

> And thou, all-shaking thunder,
> Strike flat the thick rotundity o' the world!
> Crack nature's moulds, all germens spill at once
> That make ingrateful man!
>
> (III. ii. 6–9)

When Lear in his madness is beginning to learn what he really is in relation to the universe, he asks, 'What is the cause of thunder?' (III. iv. 159), and it is from the force of thunder that Cordelia rescues him:

> Was this a face
> To be expos'd against the warring winds?
> To stand against the deep dread-bolted thunder?
>
> (IV. vii. 31–3)

The star motif which in *The Atheist's Tragedy* accompanies that of thunder is of crucial importance in *King Lear* as well. As in Tourneur's play, the stars are symbols of divine providence, and one of the questions to be debated in *King Lear* is whether or not they exercise a control over human affairs which is benevolent and just. One conventional and orthodox position is stated by Glouces-ter at the beginning of *King Lear* (I. ii. 115–28) and countered by Edmund as 'the excellent foppery of the world' (I. ii. 132 ff.) in terms which look forward to those of D'Amville (II. iv. 136–40). Allusions to the stars appear in various dramatic contexts through-out the play, as, for instance, when Kent, unable to account for a world which could produce a Goneril and Regan as well as a Cor-delia, cries out in desperation:

E

It is the stars,
The stars above us, govern our conditions.
(IV. iii. 34–5)

Tourneur's play is of a far more limited intellectual range than Shakespeare's, where there is a deep probing of such moral propositions as Tourneur takes for granted, and where there is a constant examination of them in terms of their contraries and in the light of credible human experience. Shakespeare cannot offer so simple an answer to 'What is the cause of thunder?' as Tourneur's. It is nevertheless interesting that for the dominant poetic imagery of his play Tourneur should choose symbols of such prominence in *King Lear*, and this fact leaves little doubt of the influence upon him of the greater artist.

Tourneur was neither Marlowe nor Shakespeare, and his achievement cannot be judged by their standards. Although he learned much from Shakespeare and had before him the example of Chapman and perhaps Marlowe as well, he created in *The Atheist's Tragedy* a vehicle for his own vision of reality, a kind of drama uniquely his own, and which when considered on its own terms is not among the least noteworthy achievements of its age.

THE ATHEIST'S TRAGEDY

The Names and Qualities of the Actors.

MONTFERRERS, *a baron.*
BELFOREST, *a baron.*
D'AMVILLE, *brother to Montferrers.*
LEVIDULCIA, *Lady to Belforest.*
CASTABELLA, *daughter to Belforest.*   5
CHARLEMONT, *son to Montferrers.*
ROUSARD, *elder son to D'Amville.*
SEBASTIAN, *younger son to D'Amville.*
LANGUEBEAU SNUFFE, *a Puritan, Chaplain to Belforest.*
BORACHIO, *D'Amville's instrument.*   10
CATAPLASMA, *a maker of periwigs and attires.*
SOQUETTE, *a seeming gentlewoman to Cataplasma.*
FRESCO, *servant to Cataplasma.*
Other servants.
Sergeant in war.   15
Soldiers.
Watchmen.
Officers.
Doctor.
Judges.   20
Keeper of the prison.
Executioner.

---

9. *Chaplain*] *Q (corrected); a Chaplaine Q (uncorrected).*   11. *a . . . attires*]
Q (corrected); an Attiremaker Q (uncorrected).   19. *Doctor*] *Nicoll; not in
Q.*   20. *Judges*] *centered in Q (corrected); in right hand column in Q (uncorrected).*   21. *Keeper of the prison*] *This ed.; not in Q.*   22. *Executioner*]
This ed.; not in Q.

---

3. *D'AMVILLE*] Tourneur's fondness for allegory, as Nicoll notes,
appears markedly in his choice of names. This appears to combine the
English 'vile' with the French 'D'Ame' to mean 'of evil spirit'. In 'damn',
aside from its possible echo of Chapman's 'D'Ambois' (cf. above, p. xxiv),
is an indication of the villain's fate.
   4. *LEVIDULCIA*] light and sweet.
   5. *CASTABELLA*] chaste and beautiful.
   9. *LANGUEBEAU*] beautiful tongue.
   10. *BORACHIO*] drunkard, from the Spanish 'boracho'.
instrument] tool.

2

11. *CATAPLASMA*] poultice, from the Greek κατάπλασμα.

12. *SOQUETTE*] This name may derive from the Italian verb 'soqqua-drare', to throw into confusion.

13. *FRESCO*] fresh.

15. Sergeant in war] This military title does not appear to occur else-where. Perhaps Tourneur wishes to differentiate this soldier from the sergeant (sheriff's officer) of III. ii. 82.

The Atheist's Tragedy,

or, The Honest Man's Revenge

Act I

[I. i]

Enter D'AMVILLE, BORACHIO, attended.

D'Am. I saw my nephew Charlemont but now
    Part from his father. Tell him I desire
    To speak with him.   *Exit* Servant.
                Borachio, thou art read
    In Nature and her large philosophy.
    Observ'st thou not the very self same course   5
    Of revolution both in man and beast?
Bor. The same, for birth, growth, state, decay and death;
    Only a man's beholding to his Nature
    For th' better composition o' the two.
D'Am. But where that favour of his Nature is   10
    Not full and free, you see a man becomes
    A fool, as little-knowing as a beast.
Bor. That shows there's nothing in a man above
    His Nature; if there were, consid'ring 'tis

Act I] Actus primi Scena prima. *Q.*

---

    3. *read*] learned.
    6. *revolution*] change wrought by time. Cf. Shakespeare, *2 Henry IV*,
III. i. 45–7:

> O God! that one might read the book of fate,
> And see the revolution of the times
> Make mountains level.

    7. *state*] worldly position.
    9. *composition*] combination.
    10. *favour*] advantage.

His being's excellency, 'twould not yield   15
    To Nature's weakness.

D'Am.   Then if death casts up
    Our total sum of joy and happiness,
    Let me have all my senses feasted in
    Th' abundant fulness of delight at once,
    And with a sweet insensible increase   20
    Of pleasing surfeit melt into my dust.

Bor. That revolution is too short methinks.
    If this life comprehends our happiness,
    How foolish to desire to die so soon!
    And if our time runs home unto the length   25
    Of Nature, how improvident it were
    To spend our substance on a minute's pleasure,
    And after live an age in misery!

D'Am. So thou conclud'st that pleasure only flows
    Upon the stream of riches.

Bor.   Wealth is lord   30
    Of all felicity.

D'Am.   'Tis oracle,
    For what's a man that's honest without wealth?

Bor. Both miserable and contemptible.

D'Am. He's worse, Borachio. For if charity
    Be an essential part of honesty   35
    And should be practis'd first upon ourselves,
    Which must be granted, then your honest man
    That's poor is most dishonest, for he is
    Uncharitable to the man whom he
    Should most respect. But what doth this touch me,   40

---

15. *excellency*] highest property.
16. *Nature's weakness*] i.e., death.
casts up] sums up.
22. *revolution*] Cf. I. i. 6.
25. *runs home unto*] lasts as long as (i.e., if we live as long as man can expect).
31. *oracle*] i.e., wisdom.
40. *respect*] consider, take into account (*O.E.D.*).

That seem to have enough ? Thanks industry,
'Tis true. Had not my body spread itself
Into posterity, perhaps I should
Desire no more increase of substance than
Would hold proportion with mine own dimensions.   45
Yet even in that sufficiency of state
A man has reason to provide and add,
For what is he hath such a present eye
And so prepar'd a strength that can foresee
And fortify his substance and himself   50
Against those accidents, the least whereof
May rob him of an age's husbandry ?
And for my children, they are as near to me
As branches to the tree whereon they grow,
And may as numerously be multiply'd.   55
As they increase, so should my providence,
For from my substance they receive the sap
Whereby they live and flourish.

Bor.   Sir, enough.
I understand the mark whereat you aim.

Enter CHARLEMONT.

D'Am. Silence. W' are interrupted. Charlemont!   60
Char. Good morrow, uncle.
D'Am.   Noble Charlemont,
Good morrow. Is not this the honour'd day

41. industry,] *This ed.;* industrie. *Q.*

---

41. *Thanks*] thanks to.
45. *hold proportion with*] be appropriate to.
dimensions] bodily parts. Cf. Shakespeare, *King Lear*, I. ii. 7–8 :
  When my dimensions are as well compact,
  My mind as generous, and my shape as true.
46. *sufficiency of state*] adequacy of wealth and social position.
48. *present*] prompt to perceive.
52. *husbandry*] careful management.
56. *providence*] prudent management. There is irony in the atheist's use of this term, commonly employed in the religious sense of God's foreseeing care for his creatures. Cf. also I. i. 112, I. ii. 51, and V. ii. 71.
59. *mark*] target.

    You purpos'd to set forward to the war?

Char. My inclination did intend it so.

D'Am. And not your resolution?

Char.   Yes, my lord,   65
    Had not my father contradicted it.

D'Am. O noble war, thou first original
    Of all man's honour! How dejectedly
    The baser spirit of our present time
    Hath cast itself below the ancient worth   70
    Of our forefathers, from whose noble deeds
    Ignobly we derive our pedigrees.

Char. Sir, tax not me for his unwillingness.
    By the command of his authority
    My disposition's forc'd against itself.   75

D'Am. Nephew, you are the honour of our blood.
    The troop of gentry whose inferior worth
    Should second your example are become
    Your leaders, and the scorn of their discourse
    Turns smiling back upon your backwardness.   80

Char. You need not urge my spirit by disgrace;
    'Tis free enough. My father hinders it.
    To curb me, he denies me maintenance
    To put me in the habit of my rank.
    Unbind me from that strong necessity,   85
    And call me coward if I stay behind.

D'Am. For want of means? Borachio, where's the gold?
    I'd disinherit my posterity
    To purchase honour. 'Tis an interest
    I prize above the principal of wealth.   90
    I'm glad I had th' occasion to make known
    How readily my substance shall unlock

---

68. honour! How] *This ed.;* honour. How *Q, Nicoll;* honour, how *Collins.*

    Itself to serve you. Here's a thousand crowns.
Char. My worthy uncle, in exchange for this
    I leave my bond. So I am doubly bound,   95
    By that for the repayment of this gold,
    And by this gold to satisfy your love.   *charity*
D'Am. Sir, 'tis a witness only of my love,
    And love doth always satisfy itself.
    Now to your father; labour his consent.   100
    My importunity shall second yours.
    We will obtain it.
Char.   If entreaty fail,
    The force of reputation shall prevail.   *Exit.*
D'Am. Go call my sons that they may take their leaves
    Of noble Charlemont. Now, my Borachio!   105
Bor. The substance of our former argument
    Was wealth.
D'Am.   The question how to compass it.
Bor. Young Charlemont is going to the war.
D'Am. O, thou begin'st to take me.
Bor.   Mark me then.
    Methinks the pregnant wit of man might make   110
    The happy absence of this Charlemont
    A subject for commodious providence.
    He has a wealthy father, ready ev'n
    To drop into his grave, and no man's power
    When Charlemont is gone can interpose   115
    'Twixt you and him.
D'Am.   Th' hast apprehended—both
    My meaning and my love. Now let thy trust
    For undertaking and for secrecy
    Hold measure with thy amplitude of wit,

---

100. *labour*] endeavour to bring about.
107. *compass*] accomplish.
109. *take*] understand.
111. *happy*] fortunate.
112. *providence*] Cf. I. i. 56.
118. *undertaking*] readiness to engage in dangerous work (*O.E.D.*).

And thy reward shall parallel thy worth.   120
Bor. My resolution has already bound
    Me to your service.
D'Am.   And my heart to thee.

        Enter ROUSARD *and* SEBASTIAN.

Here are my sons. . . .
There's my eternity. My life in them
And their succession shall for ever live,   125
And in my reason dwells the providence
To add to life as much of happiness.
Let all men lose, so I increase my gain:
I have no feeling of another's pain.

        easy, almost emblematic
        irony in this opening scene.
        Exeunt. D'Amville as
        *atheist machiavel is
        sitting duck for
        moral criticism*

[I. ii]

     Enter old MONTFERRERS *and* CHARLEMONT.

Mont. I prithee let this current of my tears
    Divert thy inclination from the war,
    For of my children thou art only left
    To promise a succession to my house,
    And all the honour thou canst get by arms   5
    Will give but vain addition to thy name,
    Since from thy ancestors thou dost derive
    A dignity sufficient, and as great
    As thou hast substance to maintain and bear.
    I prithee stay at home.
Char.   My noble father,   10
    The weakest sigh you breathe hath power to turn
    My strongest purpose, and your softest tear
    To melt my resolution to as soft
    Obedience. But my affection to the war

        *in contrast to D'A, M
        really believes in honor*

        *audience may be
        ambivalent re honor & war*

I. ii. 3. art] *Collins;* are *Q.*

---

126. *reason*] Cf. Introduction, p. xlviii.

I. ii. 4. *succession*] Montferrers' concern with his posterity echoes and
parallels that of D'Amville, I. i. 53–8.

Is as hereditary as my blood   15
To ev'ry life of all my ancestry.
Your predecessors were your precedents,
And you are my example. Shall I serve
For nothing but a vain parenthesis
I' th' honour'd story of your family,   20
Or hang but like an empty scutcheon
Between the trophies of my predecessors
And the rich arms of my posterity?
There's not a Frenchman of good blood and youth,
But either out of spirit or example   25
Is turn'd a soldier. Only Charlemont
Must be reputed that same heartless thing
That cowards will be bold to play upon.

        Enter D'AMVILLE, ROUSARD *and* SEBASTIAN.

D'Am. Good morrow, my lord.
Mont. Morrow, good brother.   30
Char. Good morrow, uncle.
D'Am. Morrow, kind nephew.
    What, ha' you wash'd your eyes wi' tears this morning?
    [*To* MONTFERRERS] Come, by my soul, his purpose does
        deserve
    Your free consent. Your tenderness dissuades him.   35
    What to the father of a gentleman
    Should be more tender than the maintenance
    And the increase of honour to his house?
    My lord, here are my boys. I should be proud
    That either this were able or that inclin'd   40
    To be my nephew's brave competitor.

---

24. youth] *Q* (*corrected*); youth' *Q* (*uncorrected*).

15–16. *as . . . ancestry*] i.e., as much my inheritance (from all my ances-
tors) as is my blood.
    28. *play upon*] make sport of.
    35. *tenderness*] over-concern.
    37. *tender*] precious.
    41. *competitor*] partner or associate.

Mont. Your importunities have overcome.
    Pray God my forc'd grant prove not ominous.
D'Am. [*Aside to* CHARLEMONT] We have obtain'd it.
                [*To* MONTFERRERS] Ominous ? in what ?
    It cannot be in anything but death,   45
    And I am of a confident belief
    That ev'n the time, place, manner of our deaths
    Do follow fate with that necessity
    That makes us sure to die. And in a thing
    Ordain'd so certainly unalterable,   50
    What can the use of providence prevail ?

    [*Enter*] BELFOREST, LEVIDULCIA, [*and*] CASTABELLA, *attended.*

Bel. Morrow, my Lord Montferrers, Lord D'Amville.
    Good morrow, gentlemen. Cousin Charlemont,
    Kindly good morrow. Troth, I was afear'd
    I should ha' come too late to tell you that   55
    I wish your undertakings a success
    That may deserve the measure of their worth.
Char. My lord, my duty would not let me go
    Without receiving your commandments.
Bel. Accompliments are more for ornament   60
    Than use. We should employ no time in them
    But what our serious business will admit.
Mont. Your favour had by his duty been prevented
    If we had not withheld him in the way.
D'Am. He was a-coming to present his service.   65
    But now no more. The cook invites to breakfast.

---

65. a-coming] *This ed.;* o'comming *Q, Nicoll;* a coming *Collins.*

---

    51. *providence*] the making of provisions for the future. Cf. i. i. 56.
    60. *Accompliments*] compliments, although, as Nicoll points out, the
word is used more commonly to mean 'accomplishments'. Cf. *Edward III*,
IV. iv. 66–7:
        A puissant host of men
        Array'd and fenc'd in all accompliments.
    63. *favour*] kind act, i.e., the compliment of coming to give him good
wishes.

Will't please your lordship enter ? Noble lady!

[*Exeunt all except*] CHARLEMONT *and* CASTABELLA.

Char. My noble mistress, this accompliment
　Is like an elegant and moving speech
　Compos'd of many sweet persuasive points   70
　Which second one another with a fluent
　Increase and confirmation of their force,
　Reserving still the best until the last,
　To crown the strong impulsion of the rest
　With a full conquest of the hearer's sense—   75
　Because th' impression of the last we speak
　Doth always longest and most constantly
　Possess the entertainment of remembrance.
　So all that now salute my taking leave
　Have added numerously to the love   80
　Wherewith I did receive their courtesy.
　But you, dear mistress, being the last and best
　That speaks my farewell, like th' imperious close
　Of a most sweet oration, wholly have
　Possess'd my liking and shall ever live   85
　Within the soul of my true memory.
　So, mistress, with this kiss I take my leave.

Cast. My worthy servant, you mistake th' intent
　Of kissing. 'Twas not meant to separate
　A pair of lovers, but to be the seal   90
　Of love, importing by the joining of
　Our mutual and incorporated breaths
　That we should breathe but one contracted life.
　Or stay at home, or let me go with you.

67.1. *Exeunt all except*] Symonds; *Manent Q.*

---

　70. *points*] ideas.
　71. *second*] support.
　73. *still*] always.
　74. *impulsion*] attack (upon the hearer's senses).
　80. *numerously*] abundantly.
　83. *imperious*] commanding.
　93. *contracted*] (*a*) combined, (*b*) betrothed.
　94. *Or*] either.

Char. My Castabella! For myself to stay   95
          Or you to go would either tax my youth
          With a dishonourable weakness or
          Your loving purpose with immodesty.

          Enter LANGUEBEAU SNUFFE.

          And for the satisfaction of your love,
          Here comes a man whose knowledge I have made   100
          A witness to the contract of our vows,
          Which my return, by marriage, shall confirm.
Lang. I salute you both with the spirit of copulation. I am
          already informed of your matrimonial purposes and will
          be a testimony to the integrity of your promises.   105
Cast. O the sad trouble of my fearful soul!
          My faithful servant! Did you never hear
          That when a certain great man went to th' war
          The lovely face of Heav'n was mask'd with sorrow,
          The sighing winds did move the breast of earth,   110
          The heavy clouds hung down their mourning heads
          And wept sad showers the day that he went hence,
          As if that day presag'd some ill success
          That fatally should kill his happiness,
          And so it came to pass. Methinks my eyes,   115
          Sweet Heav'n forbid, are like those weeping clouds,
          And as their showers presag'd, so do my tears,
          Some sad event will follow my sad fears.
Char. Fie, superstitious! Is it bad to kiss?
Cast. May all my fears hurt me no more than this. [*They kiss.*] 120

103–5. I . . . promises] *Q (corrected);* I . . . copulation, / I . . . matrimoniall /
Purposes . . . integritie *Q (uncorrected, first state);* I . . . am / already . . .
a / testimonie . . . integritie *Q (uncorrected, second state).*

---

96. *tax*] censure, accuse.
103–5. *I . . . promises*] On the three states of this speech, see Introduction,
pp. xxviii–xxix. Snuffe throughout the play speaks in a jargon associated
with Puritans and burlesqued in anti-Puritan satire. Cf. W. P. Holden,
Anti-Puritan Satire 1572–1642 (New Haven, 1954), particularly pp. 107–8.
108. *certain great man*] a possible personal allusion, identified by some
scholars as Sir Francis Vere. Cf. Introduction, p. xxiv.

Lang. Fie, fie, fie, these carnal kisses do stir up the concu-
    piscences of the flesh.

Enter BELFOREST *and* LEVIDULCIA.

Lev. O, here's your daughter under her servant's lips.
Char. Madam, there is no cause you should mistrust
    The kiss I gave; 'twas but a parting one.   125
Lev. A lusty blood! Now, by the lip of Love,
    Were I to choose, your joining one for me.
Bel. Your father stays to bring you on the way.
    Farewell. The Great Commander of the war
    Prosper the course you undertake. Farewell.   130
Char. My lord, I humbly take my leave. [*To* LEVIDULCIA] Madam,
    I kiss your hand. [*To* CASTABELLA] And your sweet lip.
      Farewell.
    [*Exeunt all except*] CHARLEMONT *and* LANGUEBEAU [SNUFFE].
    Her power to speak is perish'd in her tears.
    Something within me would persuade my stay,
    But reputation will not yield unto 't.   135
    Dear sir, you are the man whose honest trust
    My confidence hath chosen for my friend.
    I fear my absence will discomfort her.
    You have the power and opportunity
    To moderate her passion. Let her grief   140
    Receive that friendship from you, and your love
    Shall not repent itself of courtesy.
Lang. Sir, I want words and protestation to insinuate into
    your credit, but in plainness and truth, I will qualify her
    grief with the spirit of consolation.   145

---

127. me.] *Q, Nicoll;* me— *Collins.*   132.1. *Exeunt all except*] *This ed.;*
Manent Q.

---

    127. *joining . . . me*] 'Joining', as Nicoll indicates, is in apposition to
'parting' in line 125. The sense is that she would prefer his joining kiss to
his parting one, were the choice hers. Collins misinterprets and hence mis-
punctuates the line.
    128. *bring . . . way*] escort you.
    144. *qualify*] moderate or mitigate.

Char. Sir, I will take your friendship up at use.
  And fear not that your profit shall be small;
  Your interest shall exceed your principal.   *Exit.*

  Enter D'AMVILLE *and* BORACHIO.

D'Am. Monsieur Languebeau, happily encountered. The
  honesty of your conversation makes me request more   150
  int'rest in your familiarity.
Lang. If your lordship will be pleased to salute me without
  ceremony, I shall be willing to exchange my service for
  your favour, but this worshipping kind of entertainment
  is a superstitious vanity; in plainness and truth I love it   155
  not.
D'Am. I embrace your disposition and desire to give you as
  liberal assurance of my love as my Lord Belforest, your
  deserved favourer.
Lang. His lordship is pleased with my plainness and truth of   160
  conversation.
D'Am. It cannot displease him. In the behaviour of his noble
  daughter Castabella a man may read her worth and your
  instruction.
Lang. That gentlewoman is most sweetly modest, fair,   165
  honest, handsome, wise, well-born, and rich.
D'Am. You have given me her picture in small.
Lang. She's like your diamond, a temptation in every man's
  eye, yet not yielding to any light impression herself.
D'Am. The praise is hers, but the comparison your own.   170
                        Gives him the ring.
Lang. You shall forgive me that, sir.
D'Am. I will not do so much at your request as forgive you it.

---

146. *take . . . use*] i.e., borrow your friendship as I would money, on
terms of interest (use). On the commercial imagery in the play, see Introduction, pp. lx–lxi.
  149–51. *Monsieur . . . familiarity*] D'Amville addresses Snuffe in his own
Puritan jargon.
  167. *in small*] in few words.
  169. *light*] with a pun on 'wanton'.

F

I will only give you it, sir. By — you will make me swear.

Lang. O, by no means. Profane not your lips with the foulness
of that sin. I will rather take it. To save your oath, you   175
shall lose your ring—Verily, my lord, my praise came
short of her worth. She exceeds a jewel. This is but only
for ornament, she both for ornament and use.

D'Am. Yet unprofitably kept without use. She deserves a
worthy husband, sir. I have often wished a match be-   180
tween my elder son and her. The marriage would join
the houses of Belforest and D'Amville into a noble
alliance.

Lang. And the unity of families is a work of love and charity.

D'Am. And that work an employment well becoming the   185
goodness of your disposition.

Lang. If your lordship please to impose it upon me, I will
carry it without any second end, the surest way to satisfy
your wish.

D'Am. Most joyfully accepted.—Rousard! Here are letters   190
to my Lord Belforest touching my desire to that purpose.

Enter ROUSARD, *sickly.*

Rousard, I send you a suitor to Castabella. To this
gentleman's discretion I commit the managing of your
suit. His good success shall be most thankful to your
trust. Follow his instructions; he will be your leader.   195

Lang. In plainness and truth.

Rous. My leader? Does your lordship think me too weak to
give the onset myself?

Lang. I will only assist your proceedings.

Rous. To say true, so I think you had need, for a sick man can   200
hardly get a woman's good will without help.

---

188. *second end*] ulterior motive.

190. *Rousard*] D'Amville apparently turns and calls to Rousard who is
off stage, and then resumes his conversation with Languebeau Snuffe.

194–5. *thankful . . . trust*] i.e., advantageous as a result of your trusting
him.

Lang. Charlemont, thy gratuity and my promises were both
      but words, and both like words shall vanish into air.
      For thy poor empty hand I must be mute;
      This gives me feeling of a better suit.   205
                    Exeunt LANGUEBEAU [SNUFFE] *and* ROUSARD.
D'Am. Borachio, didst precisely note this man?
Bor. His own profession would report him pure.
D'Am. And seems to know if any benefit
      Arises of religion after death;
      Yet but compare 's profession with his life;   210
      They so directly contradict themselves
      As if the end of his instructions were
      But to divert the world from sin that he
      More easily might engross it to himself.
      By that I am confirm'd an atheist.   215
      Well, Charlemont is gone, and here thou see'st
      His absence the foundation of my plot.
Bor. He is the man whom Castabella loves.
D'Am. That was the reason I propounded him
      Employment fix'd upon a foreign place,   220
      To draw his inclination out o' th' way.
Bor. 'T has left the passage of our practice free.

---

202. *gratuity*] kindness (*O.E.D.*).
207. *profession*] declared belief, particularly with respect to religion. Cf.
Marlowe, *The Jew of Malta* (ed. Brooke), 351–3:
                    Out, wretched *Barabas*,
              Sham'st thou not thus to justify thy selfe
              As if we knew not thy profession?
210–15. *Yet . . . atheist*] Among the causes of atheism according to Elizabethan apologists was the zeal of Puritans and the corruption of the clergy.
Cf. Jeremy Corderoy, *A Warning for Worldlings* (1609) [Sig. A9]:
    First, our ouermuch patience toward them wherin (to vse his words)
    the zeale of Babel towards the glory of God, hath exceeded the zeale of
    Sion. . . . Vnto which causes, I would I might not iustly adde another,
    namely the corrupt life of some who have consecrated themselves to the
    seruice of God, yet dare not open their mouthes against corruption in
    manners.
214. *engross*] collect from all quarters (*O.E.D.*).
221. *draw . . . way*] i.e., remove him and his affection from Castabella.

D'Am. This Castabella is a wealthy heir,
  And by her marriage with my elder son
  My house is honour'd and my state increas'd.   225
  This work alone deserves my industry,
  But if it prosper thou shalt see my brain
  Make this but an induction to a point
  So full of profitable policy
  That it would make the soul of honesty   230
  Ambitious to turn villain.

Bor.   I bespeak
  Employment in 't. I'll be an instrument
  To grace performance with dexterity.

D'Am. Thou shalt. No man shall rob thee of the honour.
  Go presently and buy a crimson scarf   235
  Like Charlemont's. Prepare thee a disguise
  I' th' habit of a soldier, hurt and lame,
  And then be ready at the wedding feast,
  Where thou shalt have employment in a work
  Will please thy disposition.

Bor.   As I vow'd,   240
  Your instrument shall make your project proud.

D'Am. This marriage will bring wealth. If that succeed,
  I will increase it though my brother bleed.   *Exeunt.*

223–5. *This . . . increas'd*] D'Amville is thinking of the dowry which
Belforest will pay his son, thus increasing the estate which Rousard finally
will possess. For D'Amville to have inherited Belforest's estate through his
daughter-in-law would have been contrary to English common law. Cf.
Clarkson and Warren, p. 218.

225. *state*] estate.

228. *induction*] preliminary.

point] goal or objective. Cf. Shakespeare, *Coriolanus*, II. ii. 43–4:
                    . . . it remains,
          As the main point of this our after-meeting.

229. *policy*] This word had acquired a strong pejorative sense by Tourneur's time and was used to refer to the cunning manipulation of events
for one's own profit and delight. It was associated with popular belief about
the doctrine of Machiavelli. Cf. Napoleone Orsini, ' "Policy" or the Language of Elizabethan Machiavellianism', *Jour. of the Warburg and Cour-
tauld Institutes*, IX (1946), 122–34.

233. *grace*] adorn.   241. *instrument*] tool.

[I. iii]

Enter CASTABELLA, *avoiding the importunity of* ROUSARD.

Cast. Nay, good sir; in troth if you knew how little it pleases
    me, you would forbear it.

Rous. I will not leave thee till th' hast entertained me for thy
    servant.

Cast. My servant? You are sick you say. You would tax me of   5
    indiscretion to entertain one that is not able to do me
    service.

Rous. The service of a gentlewoman consists most in chamber
    work, and sick men are fittest for the chamber. I prithee
    give me a favour.   10

Cast. Methinks you have a very sweet favour of your own.

Rous. I lack but your black eye.

Cast. If you go to buffets among the boys, they'll give you one.

Rous. Nay, if you grow bitter I'll dispraise your black eye.
    The gray-eyed morning makes the fairest day.   15

Cast. Now that you dissemble not, I could be willing to give
    you a favour. What favour would you have?

Rous. Any toy, any light thing.

Cast. Fie! Will you be so uncivil to ask a light thing at a gentle-
    woman's hand?

Rous. Wilt give me a bracelet o' thy hair then?

    I. iii. 4. *servant*] suitor.

    5. *tax*] Cf. I. ii. 96.

    11. *favour*] face.

    12. *black eye*] possibly used with a sexual implication (vagina); cf. Part-
ridge, p. 109.

    13. *go to buffets*] brawl.

    15. *The ... day*] Cf. Tilley, M1169: 'By the morning one knows the day'.

    18. *toy*] (*a*) trifle, (*b*) amorous caress; cf. Partridge, p. 207.

    light] (*a*) trifling, (*b*) wanton.

    21. *bracelet o' thy hair*] commonly used as a love token. Cf. Donne, *The
Funeral* (ed. Grierson), I, 58:

        That subtile wreath of haire, which crowns my arme.

Shakespeare, *A Midsummer Night's Dream*, I. i. 32–3:

        And stol'n the impression of her fantasy

        With bracelets of thy hair, rings, gawds, conceits.

Cast. Do you want hair, sir ?

Rous. No, faith, I'll want no hair so long as I can have it for
money.

Cast. What would you do with my hair then ?   25

Rous. Wear it for thy sake, sweetheart.

Cast. Do you think I love to have my hair worn off ?

Rous. Come, you are so witty now and so sensible.   *Kisses her.*

Cast. Tush, I would I wanted one o' my senses now.

Rous. Bitter again! What's that ? Smelling ?   30

Cast. No, no, no. Why now y' are satisfied, I hope. I have
given you a favour.

Rous. What favour ? A kiss ? I prithee give me another.

Cast. Show me that I gave you then.

Rous. How should I show it ?   35

Cast. You are unworthy of a favour if you will not bestow the
keeping of it one minute.

Rous. Well, in plain terms, dost love me ? That's the purpose
of my coming.

Cast. Love you ? Yes, very well.   40

Rous. Give me thy hand upon 't.

Cast. Nay, you mistake me. If I love you very well, I must not
love you now, for now you are not very well; y' are sick.

Rous. This equivocation is for the jest now.

Cast. I speak 't as 'tis now in fashion, in earnest. But I shall not   45
be in quiet for you, I perceive, till I have given you a
favour. Do you love me ?

34. gave you] *Q;* gaue it you *Collins.*

---

22. *want*] lack.

23. *hair*] used in a double sense, (*a*) hair, (*b*) hare, Elizabethan slang for
prostitute. Cf. Shakespeare, *Romeo and Juliet*, II. iv. 144–7:

> An old hare hoar, and an old hare hoar,
>   Is very good meat in Lent:
> But a hare that is hoar, is too much for a score,
>   When it hoars ere it be spent.

27. *worn off*] (*a*) worn away, (*b*) worn by someone else.

28. *sensible*] capable of feeling.

44. *equivocation*] the deliberate use of words of ambiguous meaning, a
common form of Elizabethan humour. Cf. Shakespeare, *Hamlet*, v. i. 147–
8, *Macbeth*, II. iii. 1–24.

46. *in quiet for*] free from being troubled by.

Rous. With all my heart.

Cast. Then with all my heart I'll give you a jewel to hang in
    your ear. Hark ye—I can never love you.   *Exit.* 50

Rous. Call you this a jewel to hang in mine ear ? 'Tis no light
    favour, for I'll be sworn it comes somewhat heavily to me.
    Well, I will not leave her for all this. Methinks it animates
    a man to stand to 't when a woman desires to be rid of
    him at the first sight.   *Exit.* 55

[I. iv]

      Enter BELFOREST *and* LANGUEBEAU SNUFFE.

Bel. I entertain the offer of this match
    With purpose to confirm it presently.
    I have already mov'd it to my daughter.
    Her soft excuses savour'd at the first,
    Methought, but of a modest innocence   5
    Of blood, whose unmov'd stream was never drawn
    Into the current of affection. But when I
    Reply'd with more familiar arguments,
    Thinking to make her apprehension bold,
    Her modest blush fell to a pale dislike,   10
    And she refus'd it with such confidence
    As if she had been prompted by a love
    Inclining firmly to some other man,
    And in that obstinacy she remains.

Lang. Verily, that disobedience doth not become a child. It 15
    proceedeth from an unsanctified liberty. You will be

---

51. *light*] with the customary pun (wanton).
52. *heavily*] sadly.
54. *stand to 't*] persist.

I. iv. 3. *mov'd*] proposed.
8. *familiar*] intimate.
9. *apprehension*] understanding.
bold] confident, certain. Cf. Shakespeare, *Cymbeline*, II. iv. 1–3:
            I would I were so sure
        To win the king as I am bold her honour
        Will remain hers.

accessory to your own dishonour if you suffer it.

Bel. Your honest wisdom has advis'd me well.
Once more I'll move her by persuasive means.
If she resist, all mildness set apart,   20
I will make use of my authority.

Lang. And instantly, lest fearing your constraint her contrary
affection teach her some device that may prevent you.

Bel. To cut off ev'ry opportunity
Procrastination may assist her with,   25
This instant night she shall be married.

Lang. Best.

Enter CASTABELLA.

Cast. Please it your lordship, my mother attends
I' th' gallery and desires your conference.   *Exit* BELFOREST.
This means I us'd to bring me to your ear.   30
Time cuts off circumstance; I must be brief.
To your integrity did Charlemont
Commit the contract if his love and mine,
Which now so strong a hand seeks to divide
That if your grave advice assist me not   35
I shall be forc'd to violate my faith.

Lang. Since Charlemont's absence I have weighed his love
with the spirit of consideration, and in sincerity I find it to
be frivolous and vain. Withdraw your respect; his affec-
tion deserveth it not.   40

Cast. Good sir, I know your heart cannot profane
The holiness you make profession of
With such a vicious purpose as to break
The vow your own consent did help to make.

Lang. Can he deserve your love who, in neglect   45
Of your delightful conversation and

_____

22–3. *contrary affection*] i.e., love directed another way.
31. *circumstance*] particulars, details. Cf. Shakespeare, *King John*, II. i.
76–7:

> The interruption of their churlish drums
> Cuts off more circumstance.

In obstinate contempt of all your prayers
And tears, absents himself so far from your
Sweet fellowship, and with a purpose so
Contracted to that absence that you see   50
He purchases your separation with
The hazard of his blood and life, fearing
To want pretence to part your companies ?
'Tis rather hate that doth division move;
Love still desires the presence of his love.   55
Verily, he is not of the Family of Love.

Cast. O do not wrong him. 'Tis a generous mind
That led his disposition to the war,
For gentle love and noble courage are
So near ally'd that one begets another,   60
Or love is sister, and courage is the brother.
Could I affect him better than before,
His soldier's heart would make me love him more.

Lang. But, Castabella—

52–3. *fearing . . . companies*] i.e., being afraid that he may lack an excuse
to part from you.

55. *still*] always.

56. *Family of Love*] This was the name of a religious sect founded in
Holland around 1540, apparently by one Henry Nicholas, which by the
end of the 1580's was so rapidly increasing in England that Elizabeth's
government was forced to take measures against it. Its basic tenet was that
the essence of religion consisted of feelings of divine love and that all religious doctrine was essentially irrelevant. The sect was attacked and ridi-
culed, being often accused of sexual promiscuity and popularly called 'The
Family of Lust'. Cf. James Shirley, *The Lady of Pleasure* (1637) [Sig. B2ᵛ]:
>   And Ladies thither bound by a Subpena
>   Of *Venus*, and small *Cupids* high displeasure,
>   Tis but the family of love translated
>   Into more costly sinne.
Thomas Middleton's play *The Family of Love* was printed in 1608 as acted
by the Children of His Majesty's Revels. Ridicule of the sect appears to
have continued into the eighteenth century, for there is a probable allusion
to it in Henry Fielding's *The Author's Farce* (1730) [Sig. B6ᵛ]:
>   Sir, sir, all the Neighbours know that I have been as quiet a Woman
>   as any in the Parish. I had no Noises in my House till you came. We were
>   the Family of Love.

62. *affect*] love.

Enter LEVIDULCIA.

Lev. Tush, you mistake the way into a woman;   65
    The passage lies not through her reason but her blood.
        Exit LANGUEBEAU [SNUFFE], CASTABELLA *about to follow.*
    Nay, stay! How wouldst thou call the child
    That being rais'd with cost and tenderness
    To full ability of body and means
    Denies relief unto the parents who   70
    Bestow'd that bringing up?
Cast.   Unnatural.
Lev. Then Castabella is unnatural.
    Nature, the loving mother of us all,
    Brought forth a woman for her own relief,
    By generation to revive her age,   75
    Which, now thou hast ability and means
    Presented, most unkindly dost deny.
Cast. Believe me, mother, I do love a man.
Lev. Prefer'st th' affection of an absent love
    Before the sweet possession of a man,   80
    The barren mind before the fruitful body,
    Where our creation has no reference
    To man but in his body, being made
    Only for generation which, unless
    Our children can be gotten by conceit,   85
    Must from the body come. If reason were
    Our counsellor, we would neglect the work
    Of generation for the prodigal

---

66. *blood*] passion.
70. *relief*] aid or assistance.
77. *unkindly*] unnaturally.
82. *Where*] whereas.
85. *conceit*] imagination or fancy.
88–90. *prodigal ... life*] It was commonly believed that life was shortened
by sexual intercourse. Cf. Donne, *Farewell to Love* (ed. Grierson), I, 71:
        Ah cannot wee,
      As well as Cocks and Lyons jocund be,
        After such pleasures? Unlesse wise
      Nature decreed (since each such Act, they say,

Expense it draws us to of that which is
The wealth of life. Wise Nature, therefore, hath   90
Reserv'd for an inducement to our sense
Our greatest pleasure in that greatest work,
Which being offer'd thee, thy ignorance
Refuses for th' imaginary joy
Of an unsatisfy'd affection to   95
An absent man—whose blood once spent i' th' war,
Then he'll come home sick, lame, and impotent,
And wed thee to a torment, like the pain
Of Tantalus, continuing thy desire
With fruitless presentation of the thing   100
It loves, still mov'd and still unsatisfy'd.

Enter BELFOREST, D'AMVILLE, ROUSARD, SEBASTIAN,
    LANGUEBEAU [SNUFFE, *and others*].

Bel. Now, Levidulcia, hast thou yet prepar'd
    My daughter's love to entertain this man,
    Her husband here?
Lev.   I'm but her mother i' law;
    Yet if she were my very flesh and blood,   105
    I could advise no better for her good.
Rous. Sweet wife! Thy joyful husband thus salutes
    Thy cheek.
Cast.   My husband? O, I am betray'd.
    [*To* LANGUEBEAU SNUFFE] Dear friend of Charlemont,
        your purity

101.2. *and others*] &c. *Q.*   106. her good] *conj. Collins;* good *Q.*

Diminisheth the length of life a day)
    This, as shee would man should despise
        The sport;
Because that other curse of being short,
    And onely for a minute made to be,
Eagers desire to raise posterity.
99. *Tantalus*] the Greek hero who in Tartarus suffered torture of eternal
hunger and thirst with food and drink just beyond his reach.
    101. *mov'd*] aroused.
    104. *mother i' law*] step-mother.

Professes a divine contempt o' th' world;   110
O be not brib'd by that you so neglect,
In being the world's hated instrument,
To bring a just neglect upon yourself.

Kneel[s] from one to another.

[*To* BELFOREST] Dear father, let me but examine my
Affection. [*To* D'AMVILLE] Sir, your prudent judgment can
Persuade your son that 'tis improvident   116
To marry one whose disposition he
Did ne'er observe. [*To* ROUSARD] Good sir, I may be of
A nature so unpleasing to your mind,
Perhaps you'll curse the fatal hour wherein   120
You rashly marry'd me.

D'Am.   My Lord Belforest,
I would not have her forc'd against her choice.

Bel. Passion o' me, thou peevish girl. I charge
Thee by my blessing and th' authority
I have to claim th' obedience, marry him.   125

Cast. Now Charlemont! O my presaging tears,
This sad event hath follow'd my sad fears.

Seb. A rape, a rape, a rape!

Bel.   How now?

D'Am.   What's that?

Seb. Why what is't but a rape to force a wench
To marry, since it forces her to lie   130
With him she would not?

Lang.   Verily, his tongue
Is an unsanctified member.

Seb.   Verily,
Your gravity becomes your perish'd soul
As hoary mouldiness does rotten fruit.

Bel. Cousin, y' are both uncivil and profane.   135

D'Am. Thou disobedient villain, get thee out of my sight.
Now, by my soul, I'll plague thee for this rudeness.

---

113. *neglect*] punishment (in the sense of being denied salvation).

Bel. Come, set forward to the church.

Exeunt [all except] SEBASTIAN.

Seb. And verify the proverb—the nearer the church, the
    further from God. Poor wench, for thy sake may his   140
    ability die in his appetite, that thou beest not troubled
    with him thou lovest not. May his appetite move thy
    desire to another man, so he shall help to make himself
    cuckold. And let that man be one that he pays wages to,
    so thou shalt profit by him thou hatest. Let the chambers 145
    be matted, the hinges oiled, the curtain rings silenced,
    and the chamber-maid hold her peace at his own request,
    that he may sleep the quietlier; and in that sleep let him
    be soundly cuckolded. And when he knows it and seeks
    to sue a divorce, let him have no other satisfaction than 150
    this: *he lay by and slept; the law will take no hold of her
    because he winked at it.*   *Exit.*

138.1. *Exeunt . . .* SEBASTIAN] *Exeunt. | Manet* Sebastian *Q.*

139–40. *proverb . . . God*] Cf. Tilley, C380.

141. *ability*] sexual potency.

146. *matted*] its floors covered with rushes, as was common in seventeenth-century houses.

hinges oiled] Cf. Marston, *The Malcontent* (ed. Bullen), I. ii. 148–9:
. . . oiled hinges, and all the tongue-tied lascivious witnesses of great
creatures' wantonness.
Collins cites Aristophanes as evidence that Athenian ladies accomplished
the same effect by watering their hinges.

150. *satisfaction*] compensation at law.

152. winked] pretended not to see.

Act II

Music. A banquet. In the night. Enter D'AMVILLE, BELFOREST,
LEVIDULCIA, ROUSARD, CASTABELLA, LANGUEBEAU SNUFFE *at
one door; at the other door* CATAPLASMA *and* SOQUETTE,
ushered by FRESCO.

Lev. Mistress Cataplasma, I expected you an hour since.

Cata. Certain ladies at my house, madam, detained me;
otherwise I had attended your ladyship sooner.

Lev. We are beholding to you for your company. My lord, I
pray you bid these gentlewomen welcome; th' are my   5
invited friends.

D'Am. Gentlewomen, y' are welcome; pray sit down.

Lev. Fresco, by my Lord D'Amville's leave I prithee go into
the butt'ry. Thou sha't find some o' my men there; if they
bid thee not welcome, they are very loggerheads.   10

Fres. If your loggerheads will not, your hogsheads shall,
madam, if I get into the butt'ry.   *Exit.*

D'Am. That fellow's disposition to mirth should be our present example. Let's be grave and meditate when our
affairs require our seriousness. 'Tis out of season to be   15
heavily disposed.

Lev. We should be all wound up into the key of mirth.

D'Am. The music there!

Bel. Where's my Lord Montferrers? Tell him here's a room
attends him.   20

Act II] Actus secundi Scena prima *Q.*

---

10. *loggerheads*] blockheads, dolts. Cf. Shakespeare, *1 Henry IV*, II. iv.
4–5:
  With three or four loggerheads amongst three or four score hogsheads.

Enter MONTFERRERS.

Mont. Heaven give your marriage that I am deprived of, joy.
D'Am. My Lord Belforest, Castabella's health!

D'AMVILLE *drinks.*

Set ope the cellar doors, and let this health
Go freely round the house.—Another to
Your son, my lord, to noble Charlemont.   25
He is a soldier. Let the instruments
Of war congratulate his memory.   *Drums and trumpets.*

Enter a Servant.

Ser. My lord, here's one i' th' habit of a soldier says he is newly
returned from Ostend and has some business of import to
speak.   30
D'Am. Ostend! Let him come in. My soul foretells
He brings the news will make our music full.
My brother's joy would do 't, and here comes he
Will raise it.

Enter BORACHIO *disguised.*

Mont.   O my spirit, it does dissuade
My tongue to question him, as if it knew   35
His answer would displease.
D'Am.   Soldier, what news?
We heard a rumour of a blow you gave
The enemy.
Bor.   'Tis very true, my lord.
Bel. Canst thou relate it?
Bor.   Yes.
D'Am.   I prithee do.
Bor. The enemy, defeated of a fair   40

23. ope] *Symonds;* ope' *Q, Collins, Nicoll.*

---

27. *congratulate*] salute.
29. *Ostend*] The siege of Ostend began in 1601 and lasted until 1604. Cf.
Introduction, pp. xxiii–xxiv.
40–70. *The enemy . . . slain*] i.e., the enemy, having been cheated of an

Advantage by a flatt'ring stratagem,
Plants all th' artillery against the town,
Whose thunder and lightning made our bulwarks shake,
And threat'ned in that terrible report
The storm wherewith they meant to second it.   45
Th' assault was general, but for the place
That promis'd most advantage to be forc'd,
The pride of all their army was drawn forth
And equally divided into front
And rear. They march'd, and coming to a stand,   50
Ready to pass our channel at an ebb,
W' advis'd it for our safest course to draw
Our sluices up and make 't unpassable.
Our governor oppos'd, and suffer'd 'em
To charge us home e'en to the rampier's foot,   55
But when their front was forcing up our breach
At push o' pike, then did his policy
Let go the sluices and tripp'd up the heels
Of the whole body of their troop that stood

---

advantage by our superior strategy, directed all its artillery against the city, making the bulwarks shake, and indicating in the sound of cannon the general assault to follow. All of their soldiers were in the action, but the best of their troops were concentrated upon one point whose taking would afford them most advantage. These men were divided into a vanguard and a rear. When they stopped before the river, ready to cross it at ebb-tide, we suggested opening our floodgates so as to make it impassable. Our governor refused and permitted them to charge across the water right up to the dam behind which we waited. At this point, when their vanguard was attacking us hand-to-hand, he opened the floodgates so that the enemy troops were caught in the water. The vanguard attempted one last desperate charge, but was overcome. Of the others, those that could not swim were drowned, and those who tried to escape by swimming were shot by our troops guarding the flanks of the river.

45. *storm*] assault, with the suggestion of 'storm' in the usual sense, carrying on the image of 'thunder and lightning' from l. 43.

53. *sluices*] floodgates.

55. *rampier*] dam or barrier (*O.E.D.*), although the word is more commonly equivalent to 'rampart'.

57. *push o' pike*] hand-to-hand combat.
policy] strategy.

Within the violent current of the stream.   60
Their front, beleaguer'd 'twixt the water and
The town, seeing the flood was grown too deep
To promise them a safe retreat, expos'd
The force of all their spirits, like the last
Expiring gasp of a strong-hearted man,   65
Upon the hazard of one charge, but were
Oppress'd and fell. The rest that could not swim
Were only drown'd, but those that thought to 'scape
By swimming were by murderers that flanker'd
The level of the flood both drown'd and slain.   70

D'Am. Now by my soul, soldier, a brave service.

Mont. O what became of my dear Charlemont?

Bor. Walking next day upon the fatal shore,
Among the slaughter'd bodies of their men
Which the full-stomach'd sea had cast upon   75
The sands, it was m' unhappy chance to light
Upon a face, whose favour when it liv'd
My astonish'd mind inform'd me I had seen.
He lay in 's armour as if that had been
His coffin, and the weeping sea, like one   80
Whose milder temper doth lament the death
Of him whom in his rage he slew, runs up
The shore, embraces him, kisses his cheek,
Goes back again, and forces up the sands
To bury him, and ev'ry time it parts   85
Sheds tears upon him, till at last, as if
It could no longer endure to see the man

---

69. flanker'd] *Q, Nicoll;* flank'd *Collins.*

---

69. *flanker'd*] As Nicoll points out, 'to flanker' is an obsolete verb meaning 'to protect the flanks', the sense of the passage being that those who
thought to escape by swimming were drowned and slain by murderers who
protected the flanks of the river. Collins' emendation is unnecessary.

70. *both . . . slain*] i.e., allowed to drown after being shot (as contrasted
with those who merely drowned).

75. *full-stomach'd*] satiated.

77. *favour*] features.

G

Whom it had slain, yet loath to leave him, with
A kind of unresolv'd unwilling pace,
Winding her waves one in another, like   90
A man that folds his arms or wrings his hands
For grief, ebb'd from the body and descends,
As if it would sink down into the earth
And hide itself for shame of such a deed.

D'Am. And, soldier, who was this ?

Mont.   O Charlemont!   95

Bor. Your fear hath told you that whereof my grief
Was loath to be the messenger.

Cast.   O God.   *Exit.*

D'Am. Charlemont drown'd ? Why how could that be, since
It was the adverse party that received
The overthrow ?   100

Bor. His forward spirit press'd into the front,
And being engag'd within the enemy
When they retreated through the rising stream,
I' the violent confusion of the throng
Was overborne and perish'd in the flood.   105
And here's the sad remembrance of his life,

                    [*He shows*] *the scarf.*

Which for his sake I will for ever wear.

Mont. Torment me not with witnesses of that
Which I desire not to believe, yet must.

D'Am. Thou art a screech-owl and dost come i' night   110
To be the cursed messenger of death.
Away. Depart my house, or, by my soul,
You'll find me a more fatal enemy
Than ever was Ostend. Be gone. Dispatch.

Bor. Sir, 'twas my love.

106.1. *He . . . scarf*] *This ed.; the scarfe Q, Nicoll;* The scarfe, *Collins.*
110. i' night] *Q, Nicoll;* i' th' night *Collins;* i' the night *Symonds.*

106.1. the scarf] This is clearly a stage direction, probably a prompter's
memorandum as Nicoll points out, and not a part of the speech, as Collins
and Symonds have it.

110. *screech-owl*] a bird regarded traditionally as a creature of ill-omen.

D'Am.   Your love to vex my heart   115
          With that I hate? Hark, do you hear, you knave?
          [*Aside to* BORACHIO] O th' art a most delicate sweet elo-
          quent villain.
Bor. [*Aside to* D'AMVILLE] Was 't not well counterfeited?   *melodramsneer*
D'Am. [*Aside to* BORACHIO] Rarely. [*Aloud*] Be gone; I will not
          here reply.   120
Bor. Why then, farewell. I will not trouble you.   *Exit.*
D'Am. [*Aside*] So. The foundation's laid. Now by degrees
          The work will rise and soon be perfected.
          [*To the others*] O this uncertain state of mortal man!
Bel. What then? It is th' inevitable fate   125
          Of all things underneath the moon.
D'Am.   'Tis true.
          Brother, for health's sake overcome your grief.
Mont. I cannot, sir. I am uncapable
          Of comfort. My turn will be next. I feel
          Myself not well.
D'Am.   You yield too much to grief.   130
Lang. All men are mortal. The hour of death is uncertain.
          Age makes sickness the more dangerous, and grief is
          subject to distraction. You know not how soon you may
          be deprived of the benefit of sense. In my understanding,
          therefore, you shall do well if you be sick to set your   135
          state in present order. Make your will.
D'Am. [*Aside*] I have my wish.
          [*To the others*] Lights for my brother.
Mont.   I'll withdraw a while,
          And crave the honest counsel of this man.

---

    116. *that*] that which.
    123. *perfected*] stressed on first syllable, as usual in the seventeenth
century.
    133. *subject to*] likely to cause.
    134–6. *benefit . . . will*] In English common law the will would not be
valid if it could be proved that its maker was not in proper mental capacity
when it was drawn up. Cf. Clarkson and Warren, p. 233.
    136. *state*] estate.

Bel. With all my heart. I pray attend him, sir.   140

   Exeunt MONTFERRERS *and* [LANGUEBEAU] SNUFFE.

This next room, please your lordship.

D'Am.   Where you will.

   Exeunt BELFOREST *and* D'AMVILLE.

Lev. My daughter's gone. Come son. Mistress Cataplasma,
 come; we'll up into her chamber. I'd fain see how she
 entertains the expectation of her husband's bedfellow-
 ship.   145

Rous. 'Faith, howsoever she entertains it, I
 Shall hardly please her; therefore let her rest.

Lev. Nay, please her hardly, and you please her best.   *Exeunt.*

[II. ii]

   Enter three Servants, *drunk, drawing in* FRESCO.

1 Ser. Boy! Fill some drink, boy.

Fres. Enough, good sir; not a drop more by this light.

2 Ser. Not by this light? Why then put out the candles, and
 we'll drink i' the dark and t' wou't, old boy.

Fres. No, no, no, no, no.   5

3 Ser. Why then take thy liquor. A health, Fresco!   *Kneel*[s].

Fres. Your health will make me sick, sir.

1 Ser. Then 'twill bring you o' your knees I hope, sir.

Fres. May I not stand and pledge it, sir?

2 Ser. I hope you will do as we do.   10

II. ii. 4. t' wou't] *This ed.;* t'wut *Q, Nicoll;* to't *Collins;* t-to't *Symonds.*

---

148. *hardly*] vigorously, playing on the 'hardly' of the previous line.

II. ii. 4. *and t' wou't*] if thou wilt. The locution is a favourite with Tourneur.

6. Kneels] It was a custom for London gallants to toast their mistresses
upon their knees, after which they were dubbed 'knight'. Cf. *A Yorkshire
Tragedy* (1608) [Sig. A3^V]: 'they call it knighting in London, when they
drink vpon their knees.' Cf. also Nashe's *Summers Last Will and Testament*
(ed. McKerrow, rev. Wilson, III, 267) where Will is dubbed 'knight' by
Bacchus after drinking on his knees before him.

9. *pledge it*] drink a toast.

Fres. Nay then, indeed I must not stand, for you cannot.

3 Ser. Well said, old boy.

Fres. Old boy! You'll make me a young child anon, for if I
continue this, I shall scarce be able to go alone.

1 Ser. My body is as weak as water, Fresco.   15

Fres. Good reason, sir. The beer has sent all the malt up into
your brain and left nothing but the water in your body.

> *Enter* D'AMVILLE *and* BORACHIO, *closely observing*
> *their drunkenness.*

D'Am. Borachio, seest those fellows?

Bor.   Yes, my Lord.

D'Am. Their drunkenness that seems ridiculous
Shall be a serious instrument to bring   20
Our sober purposes to their success.

Bor. I am prepar'd for th' execution, sir.

D'Am. Cast off this habit and about it straight.

Bor. Let them drink healths and drown their brains i' the flood;
I'll promise them they shall be pledg'd in blood.   *Exit.* 25

1 Ser. You ha' left a damnable snuff here.

2 Ser. Do you take that in snuff, sir?

1 Ser. You are a damnable rogue then.

> [*They fall*] *together by th' ears.*

D'Am. [*Aside*] Fortune, I honour thee. My plot still rises
According to the model of mine own desires.   30
[*To the others*] Lights for my brother! What, ha' you
drunk yourselves mad, you knaves.

1 Ser. My lord, the jacks abused me.

---

14. *go*] walk.

24. *drown . . . flood*] Cf. Tilley, B592: 'He that fills his brain with wine
can put nothing else in it'.

26. *snuff*] a portion of drink left at the bottom of a cup (*O.E.D.*).

27. *take that in snuff*] take offence at that. Cf. Tilley, S598; Shakespeare,
1 Henry IV, I. iii. 40–1:

> Who therewith angry, when it next came there,
> Took it in snuff.

33. *jacks*] knaves.

D'Am. I think they are the jacks indeed that have abused thee.
  Dost hear ? That fellow is a proud knave. He has abused   35
  thee. As thou goest over the fields by and by in lighting
  my brother home, I'll tell thee what sha't do: knock him
  over the pate with thy torch; I'll bear thee out in 't.
1 Ser. I will singe the goose by this torch.   *Exit.*
D'Am. [*to the* Second Servant] Dost hear, fellow ? Seest thou   40
  that proud knave ? I have given him a lesson for his
  sauciness. 'Has wrong'd thee. I'll tell thee what sha't do:
  as we go over the fields by and by, clap him suddenly o'er
  the coxcomb with thy torch; I'll bear thee out in 't.
2 Ser. I will make him understand as much.   *Exit.*   45

      Enter LANGUEBEAU SNUFFE.

D'Am. Now, Monsieur Snuffe, what has my brother done ?
Lang. Made his will, and by that will made you his heir, with
  this proviso, that as occasion shall hereafter move him, he
  may revoke or alter it when he pleases.
D'Am. Yes, let him if he can.—I'll make it sure   50
  From his revoking.   *Aside.*

   Enter MONTFERRERS *and* BELFOREST, *attended with lights.*

Mont.   Brother, now good night.
D'Am. The sky is dark; we'll bring you o'er the fields.
  [*Aside*] Who can but strike wants wisdom to maintain;
  He that strikes safe and sure has heart and brain.   *Exeunt.*

---

  34. *jacks*] (*a*) knaves, (*b*) drinking jacks, large vessels, originally of waxed
leather coated on the outside with tar or pitch (*O.E.D.*).
  38. *bear thee out in 't*] support you in it. Cf. Shakespeare, *2 Henry IV,*
v. i. 52–5:
   and if I cannot once or twice in a quarter bear out a knave against an
   honest man, I have but a very little credit with your worship.
  44. *coxcomb*] head (originally a cap worn by a fool).
  53. *maintain*] persevere in it (*O.E.D.*).

[II. iii]

Enter CASTABELLA *alone.*

Cast. O love, thou chaste affection of the soul,
Without th' adult'rate mixture of the blood,
That virtue which to goodness addeth good,
The minion of Heaven's heart. Heaven, is 't my fate
For loving that thou lov'st, to get thy hate?   5
Or was my Charlemont thy chosen love,
And therefore hast receiv'd him to thyself?
Then I confess thy anger's not unjust.
I was thy rival. Yet to be divorc'd
From love has been a punishment enough,   10
Sweet Heaven, without being marry'd unto hate.
Hadst thou been pleas'd—O double misery!
Yet, since thy pleasure hath inflicted it,
If not my heart, my duty shall submit.

Enter LEVIDULCIA, ROUSARD, CATAPLASMA, SOQUETTE, *and*
FRESCO, *with a lantern.*

Lev. Mistress Cataplasma, good night. I pray when your man   15
has brought you home, let him return and light me to my
house.
Cata. He shall instantly wait on your ladyship.
Lev. Good, Mistress Cataplasma, for my servants are all
drunk; I cannot be beholding to 'em for their attendance.   20
                    Exeunt CATAPLASMA, SOQUETTE *and* FRESCO.
O here's your bride.
Rous.   And melancholic too,
Methinks.
Lev.   How can she choose? Your sickness will

II. iii. 11–12. hate. . . . pleas'd—] *This ed.;* hate, . . . pleas'd: *Q.*   19.
Good,] Good *Q.*

II. iii. 4. *minion*] darling.
5. *that thou lov'st*] i.e., him whom you love.
12. *Hadst . . . pleased*] Tourneur's sense here is not entirely clear, but it
seems most likely that this is a broken sentence, 'thou' referring to 'heaven'.

Distaste th' expected sweetness o' the night.
That makes her heavy.

Rous.   That should make her light.

Lev. Look you to that.

Cast.   What sweetness speak you of?   25
The sweetness of the night consists in rest.

Rous. With that sweetness thou shalt be surely blest
Unless my groaning wake thee. Do not moan.

Lev. Sh' had rather you would wake and make her groan.

Rous. Nay 'troth, sweetheart, I will not trouble thee.   30
Thou shalt not lose thy maidenhead tonight.

Cast. O might that weakness ever be in force,
I never would desire to sue divorce.

Rous. Wilt go to bed?

Cast.   I will attend you, sir.

Rous. Mother, good night.

Lev.   Pleasure be your bedfellow.   35
                        Exeunt ROUSARD *and* CASTABELLA.

Why sure their generation was asleep
When she begot those dormice, that she made
Them up so weakly and imperfectly.
One wants desire, the t'other ability—
When my affection even with their cold bloods,   40
As snow rubb'd through an active hand does make
The flesh to burn, by agitation is
Inflam'd! I could unbrace and entertain

29. Sh' had] *This ed.;* Sh'ad *Q, Nicoll;* She'd *Collins.*   43. unbrace] *Q;*
imbrace *Collins, Nicoll;* embrace *Symonds.*

---

23. *Distaste*] mar.
24. *heavy*] sad.
light] with the customary pun (wanton).
36. *generation was asleep*] i.e., when they were conceived, their parents
were not fully awake. Cf. Shakespeare, *King Lear*, I. ii. 15.
37. *dormice*] sleepy, inactive persons (*O.E.D.*).
40. *affection*] passion.
41. *active*] vigorous.
43. *unbrace*] undress. Cf. William Rowley, *A Match at Midnight* (1633)
[Sig. H3ʳ]:

The air to cool it.

Enter SEBASTIAN.

Seb.   That but mitigates
        The heat; rather embrace and entertain   45
        A younger brother; he can quench the fire.
Lev. Can you so, sir? Now I beshrew your ear.
        Why, bold Sebastian, how dare you approach
        So near the presence of your displeas'd father?
Seb. Under the protection of his present absence.   50
Lev. Belike you knew he was abroad then?
Seb.   Yes.
        Let me encounter you so; I'll persuade
        Your means to reconcile me to his love.
Lev. Is that the way? I understand you not.
        But for your reconcilement, meet m' at home;   55
        I'll satisfy your suit.
Seb.   Within this half hour?   *Exit.*
Lev. Or within this whole hour. When you will.—A lusty
        blood! Has both the presence and the spirit of a man. I
        like the freedom of his behaviour. Ho! Sebastian! Gone?
        Has set my blood a-boiling i' my veins, and now, like 60
        water poured upon the ground that mixes itself with
        ev'ry moisture it meets, I could clasp with any man.

        Enter FRESCO *with a lantern.*

        O Fresco, art thou come?
        If t'other fail, then thou art entertain'd.
        Lust is a spirit which whosoe'er doth raise,   65
        The next man that encounters boldly lays.   *Exeunt.*

Wid. Why what do you meane, you will not bee so uncivil to unbrace
    you here.
Alex. By these Buckles I will, and what they will thinke on 't—[and he
    proceeds to undress until the Widow agrees to marry him].
Collins' emendation, followed by Nicoll, seems hardly necessary.
    47. *ear*] i.e., for having overheard her.
    66. *lays*] (*a*) exorcises (a ghost), (*b*) has coition with.

[II. iv]

> *Enter* BORACHIO *warily and hastily over the stage, with*
> *a stone in either hand.*

Bor. Such stones men use to raise a house upon,
But with these stones I go to ruin one.   *Descends.*

> *Enter two* Servants, *drunk, fighting with their torches;* D'AMVILLE,
> MONTFERRERS, BELFOREST, *and* LANGUEBEAU SNUFFE.

Bel. Passion o' me, you drunken knaves, you'll put
The lights out.
D'Am.   No, my lord, th' are but in jest.
1 Ser. Mine's out.   5
D'Am. Then light it at his head; that's light enough.
'Fore God, th' are out. You drunken rascals, back
And light 'em.
Bel.   'Tis exceeding dark.   *Exeunt* Servants.
D'Am.   No matter;
I am acquainted with the way. Your hand.
Let's easily walk. I'll lead you till they come.   10
Mont. My soul's oppress'd with grief. 'T lies heavy at
My heart. O my departed son, ere long
I shall be with thee.
> D'AMVILLE *thrusts him down into the gravel pit.*
D'Am.   Marry, God forbid!
Mont. O, O, O.
D'Am. Now all the host of heaven forbid! Knaves! Rogues!   15
Bel. Pray God he be not hurt! He's fall'n into the gravel pit.

II. iv. 7. 'Fore God] *Collins;* Foregod *Q.*

II. iv. 0.1–2. Enter . . . hand] Borachio enters from one side of the yard, crosses the platform, speaking his two lines as he does so, and descends on the other side, where he waits in hiding for Montferrers to be thrust down to him. This area, in the yard at the side of the platform, comes to represent the gravel pit. Cf. Allardyce Nicoll, 'Passing over the Stage', *Shakespeare Survey* 12 (1959), p. 54.
  6. *light*] light-witted.
  15. *Now . . . heaven*] Cf. Shakespeare, *Hamlet*, I. v. 92:
          O all you host of heaven! O earth! What else ?

D'Am. Brother, dear brother! Rascals, villains, knaves!   Cain

Enter the Servants *with lights.*

Eternal darkness damn you; come away.
Go round about into the gravel pit,
And help my brother up. Why what a strange   20
Unlucky night is this! Is 't not, my lord?
I think that dog that howl'd the news of grief,
That fatal screech-owl, usher'd on this mischief.

Enter [Servants] *with the murdered body.*

Lang. Mischief indeed, my lord. Your brother's dead.
Bel. He's dead.
1 Ser.   He's dead.
D'Am.   Dead be your tongues! Drop out   25
Mine eye-balls, and let envious Fortune play   tsk
At tennis with 'em. Have I liv'd to this?
Malicious Nature! Hadst thou born me blind,
Th' hadst yet been something favourable to me.
No breath? No motion? Prithee tell me, Heaven,   30
Hast shut thine eye to wink at murder, or
Hast put this sable garment on to mourn
At 's death?

25. *1 Ser.*] *This ed.; Ser. Q.*

25–42. *Dead . . . destiny*] U. M. Ellis-Fermor has compared this speech
to that in Shakespeare, *Macbeth*, II. iii. 115–25. 'Each man', she writes, 'is
overacting in a crisis, the part of the horror-stricken discoverer of a murder
he has in fact himself committed' (*Jacobean Drama*, p. 161).

26–7. *Fortune . . . 'em*] Cf. Webster, *Duchess of Malfi* (ed. Lucas), v. iv.
63–4:

We are meerely the Starres tennys-balls (strooke, and banded
Which way please them).

Edward Sharpham, *Cupids Whirligig* (1607) [Sig. G3ʳ]:

Why they say the worlde is like a Byas bowle, and it runnes all on the
rich mens sides: others say, tis like a Tennis-ball, and fortune keepes
such a Racket with it, as it tosses it into times hazard.

The metaphor is a Renaissance commonplace which may go back as far as
the *Captivi* (Prol. 22) of Plautus. Cf. R. W. Dent, *Webster's Borrowing*
(Berkeley, Calif., 1960), p. 259.

Not one poor spark in the whole spacious sky
Of all that endless number would vouchsafe   35
To shine ? You viceroys to the king of Nature!
Whose constellations govern mortal births,
Where is that fatal planet rul'd at his
Nativity ? That might ha' pleas'd to light
Him out, as well into th' world, unless   40
It be asham'd t' have been the instrument
Of such a good man's cursed destiny.

Bel. Passions transports you. Recollect yourself.
Lament him not. Whether our deaths be good
Or bad, it is not death but life that tries.   45
He liv'd well, therefore questionless well dies.

D'Am. Ay, 'tis an easy thing for him that has
No pain to talk of patience. Do you think
That Nature has no feeling ?

Bel.   Feeling ? Yes.
But has she purpos'd anything for nothing ?   50
What good receives this body by your grief ?
Whether is 't more unnatural not to grieve

43. Passions] *Q;* Passion *Collins.*

34–42. *Not . . . destiny*] These lines seem to echo the fourth addition to
the 1602 *Spanish Tragedy* (ed. Edwards), p. 128:

> And yonder pale-fac'd Hecate there, the moon,
> Doth give consent to that is done in darkness,
> And all those stars that gaze upon her face
> Are aglets on her sleeve, pins on her train:
> And those that should be powerful and divine,
> Do sleep in darkness when they most should shine.

36–9. *You . . . Nativity*] Cf. Marlowe, *Doctor Faustus* (ed. Jump), xix.
157–8:

> You stars that reign'd at my nativity,
> Whose influence hath allotted death and hell.

Jump calls attention to *1 Tamburlaine*, IV. ii. 33: 'Smile, stars that reign'd
at my nativity', and to John Ford, *'Tis Pity She's a Whore*, v. i:

> Would thou hadst been less subject to those stars
> That luckless reign'd at my nativity!

45. *tries*] puts to the test.
51–4. *What . . . vain*] Cf. Shakespeare, *Hamlet*, I. ii. 87 ff.
52. *Whether*] here used as an interrogative particle introducing a disjunc-
tive direct question, expressing a doubt between two alternatives.

For him you cannot help with it, or hurt
Yourself with grieving and yet grieve in vain?
D'Am. Indeed, had he been taken from me like   55
A piece o' dead flesh, I should neither ha' felt it
Nor griev'd for 't. But come hither, pray look here.
Behold the lively tincture of his blood!
Neither the dropsy nor the jaundice in 't,
But the true freshness of a sanguine red,   60
For all the fog of this black murd'rous night
Has mix'd with it. For anything I know,
He might ha' liv'd till doomsday and ha' done
More good than either you or I. O brother!
He was a man of such a native goodness,   65
As if regeneration had been given
Him in his mother's womb, so harmless
That rather than ha' trod upon a worm
He would ha' shunn'd the way, so dearly pitiful
That ere the poor could ask his charity   70
With dry eyes, he gave 'em relief wi' tears—
With tears—yes, faith, with tears.
Bel.   Take up the corpse.
For wisdom's sake, let reason fortify
This weakness.
D'Am.   Why, what would you ha' me do?
Foolish Nature will have her course in spite   75
O' wisdom. But I have e'en done.
All these words were but a great wind, and now
This shower of tears has laid it, I am calm
Again. You may set forward when you will.
I'll follow you like one that must and would not.   80
Lang. Our opposition will but trouble him.
Bel. The grief that melts to tears by itself is spent;

---

61. *For all*] although.
68–9. *That . . . way*] Cf. Shakespeare, *Pericles*, IV. i. 78–9:
             I trod upon a worm against my will,
             But I wept for it.
78. *laid*] allayed.

Passion resisted grows more violent.

Exeunt [all except] D'AMVILLE. BORACHIO *ascends.*

D'Am. Here's a sweet comedy. 'T begins with *O*
      Dolentis and concludes with ha, ha, he.   85
Bor. Ha, ha, he.
D'Am.   O my echo! I could stand
      Reverberating this sweet musical air
      Of joy till I had perish'd my sound lungs
      With violent laughter. Lovely night-raven!
      Th' hast seiz'd a carcass.
Bor.   Put him out on 's pain.   90
      I lay so fitly underneath the bank
      From whence he fell, that ere his falt'ring tongue
      Could utter double O, I knock'd out 's brains
      With this fair ruby, and had another stone
      Just of this form and bigness ready; that   95
      I laid i' the broken skull upo' the ground
      For 's pillow, against the which they thought he fell
      And perish'd.
D'Am. Upon this ground I'll build my manor house,
      And this shall be the chiefest corner-stone.   100
Bor. 'T has crown'd the most judicious murder that
      The brain of man was e'er deliver'd of.
D'Am. Ay, mark the plot. Not any circumstance

83.1. *all except*] *Symonds; Manet Q.*   89. Lovely] *Q;* Lonely *Collins.*
93. O] *Symonds;* Oo *Q.*

83.1. ascends] He mounts from the yard to the platform.
   84–5. *begins . . .* Dolentis] 'With the O of one in pain; cf. *heus admirantis,*
etc., an odd and tragical application of a rule from Latin Grammar'
(Collins).
   88. *perish'd*] caused to perish. Cf. Shakespeare, *2 Henry VI,* III. ii. 99–
100:

        Because thy flinty heart, more hard than they,
        Might in thy palace perish Margaret.
   94. *ruby*] i.e., the stone dyed red with blood.
   103. *Ay, mark the plot*] The review of villainy which follows is the typical
confessional speech of the Machiavel gloating over the cleverness of his
crimes. Cf. Marlowe, *The Jew of Malta* (ed. Brooke), 930–66.

That stood within the reach of the design
Of persons, dispositions, matter, time,   105
Or place, but by this brain of mine was made
An instrumental help, yet nothing from
Th' induction to th' accomplishment seem'd forc'd
Or done o' purpose, but by accident.

Bor. First my report that Charlemont was dead,   110
Though false, yet cover'd with a mask of truth.

D'Am. Ay, and deliver'd in as fit a time,
When all our minds so wholly were possess'd
With one affair, that no man would suspect
A thought employ'd for any second end.   115

Bor. Then the precisian to be ready when
Your brother spake of death, to move his will.

D'Am. His business call'd him thither, and it fell
Within his office, unrequested to 't.
From him it came religiously and sav'd   120
Our project from suspicion, which if I
Had mov'd had been endanger'd.

Bor.   Then your healths,
Though seeming but the ordinary rites
And ceremonies due to festivals—

D'Am. Yet us'd by me to make the servants drunk,   125
An instrument the plot could not have miss'd.
'Twas easy to set drunkards by the ears;
Th' had nothing but their torches to fight with,
And when those lights were out—

Bor.   Then darkness did
Protect the execution of the work   130
Both from prevention and discovery.

---

128. Th' had] *This ed.;* Th'ad *Q;* They'd *Collins.*

---

108. *induction*] preparation for.
113. *possess'd*] occupied.
115. *second end*] Cf. I. ii. 188.
116–17. *precisian . . . will*] It was a common practice for clergymen to
stand ready to draft the wills of their dying parishioners. Cf. Clarkson and
Warren, p. 237.
116. *precisian*] Puritan, i.e., Languebeau Snuffe.

D'Am. Here was a murder bravely carry'd through
          The eye of observation, unobserv'd.
Bor. And those that saw the passage of it made
          The instruments, yet knew not what they did.   135
D'Am. That power of rule philosophers ascribe
          To him they call the supreme of the stars,
          Making their influences governors
          Of sublunary creatures, when their selves
          Are senseless of their operations—   *Thunder and lightning.*
                                        What!   140
          Dost start at thunder ? Credit my belief,
          'Tis a mere effect of Nature,
          An exhalation hot and dry, involv'd
          Within a wat'ry vapour i' the middle
          Region of the air, whose coldness   145
          Congealing that thick moisture to a cloud,
          The angry exhalation shut within
          A prison of contrary quality,
          Strives to be free, and with the violent
          Eruption through the grossness of that cloud   150
          Makes this noise we hear.
Bor.   'Tis a fearful noise.

145. Region] *Collins;* religion *Q.*

132–3. *carry'd . . . observation*] done before witnesses.
136–40. *That . . . operations*] Cf. Shakespeare, *King Lear,* I. ii. 132–49.
139. *sublunary*] earthly (beneath the moon), as opposed to celestial.
141–51. *Credit . . . hear*] Collins attributes this explanation of thunder to Lucretius, *De Rerum Natura,* VI, 270 ff., but cf. Leonard Digges, *A Prognostication euerlastinge of righte good effect* (1576) [Sig. DI^v]:
          Thunder is the quenching of fyre, in a cloude. Or thunder is an exhalation, hot and dry, mixt with moisture caryed vp to the middle Region, there thicked and wrapped into a cloud, of this hotte matter coupled in moystnes, closed in the cloud, groweth a strife, the heate beatinge, and breaking out the sides of ye cloude wyth a thundringe noyse: the fyre then dispersed, is the lightninge.
This explanation, which may go back to Aristotle's *Meteorologia,* 363, appears also in Thomas Hill, *A Contemplation of mysteries* (1571), p. 53, and in Simon Harward, *A Discourse of the Severall Kinds and Causes of Lightnings* (1607) [Sig. C3^r–C3^v]. (I owe this note to Professor William Elton.)

D'Am. 'Tis a brave noise,
　　And methinks graces our accomplished
　　Project as a peal of ordnance
　　Does a triumph; it speaks encouragement.　　　155
　　Now Nature shows thee how it favour'd our
　　Performance, to forbear this noise when we
　　Set forth because it should not terrify
　　My brother's going home, which would have dash'd
　　Our purpose—to forbear this lightning　　　160
　　In our passage, lest it should ha' warn'd him
　　O' the pitfall. Then propitious Nature wink'd
　　At our proceedings; now it doth express
　　How that forbearance favour'd our success.

Bor. You have confirm'd me, for it follows well　　　165
　　That Nature, since herself decay doth hate,
　　Should favour those that strengthen their estate.

D'Am. Our next endeavour is—since on the false
　　Report that Charlemont is dead depends
　　The fabric of the work—to credit that　　　170
　　With all the countenance we can.

Bor.　　　　　　　　　　　　Faith, sir,
　　Even let his own inheritance, whereof
　　Y' have dispossess'd him, countenance the act.
　　Spare so much out of that to give him a
　　Solemnity of funeral; 'twill quit　　　175
　　The cost and make your apprehension of

168. is—] is; *Q.*　　170. work—] work; *Q.*

---

154. *ordnance*] here pronounced as trisyllabic.
155. *triumph*] victorious entrance of a military commander, or other public celebration of victory.
160. *lightning*] here pronounced as trisyllabic.
161. *passage*] journey.
162–3. *wink'd At*] seemed not to see, acquiesced in.
165. *confirm'd*] convinced.
170. *credit*] accredit.
171. *countenance*] feigned appearance, pretence (*O.E.D.*).
173. *countenance*] support.
175–6. *quit . . . cost*] be worth the expense.
176. *apprehension*] Cf. I. iv. 9.

H

His death appear more confident and true.

D'Am. I'll take thy counsel. Now farewell black night,
  Thou beauteous mistress of a murderer;
  To honour thee, that hast accomplish'd all,   180
  I'll wear thy colours at his funeral.   *Exeunt.*

[II. v]

  Enter LEVIDULCIA *into her chamber, manned by* FRESCO.

Lev. Th' art welcome into my chamber, Fresco. Prithee shut
  the door.—Nay, thou mistakest me. Come in and shut it.
Fres. 'Tis somewhat late, madam.
Lev. No matter. I have somewhat to say to thee.
  What, is not thy mistress towards a husband yet?   5
Fres. Faith, madam, she has suitors, but they will not suit her,
  methinks. They will not come off lustily, it seems.
Lev. They will not come on lustily, thou wouldst say.
Fres. I mean, madam, they are not rich enough.
Lev. But ay, Fresco, they are not bold enough. Thy mistress is 10
  of a lively attractive blood, Fresco, and in troth she's o'
  my mind for that. A poor spirit is poorer than a poor
  purse. Give me a fellow that brings not only temptation
  with him, but has the activity of wit and audacity of spirit
  to apply every word and gesture of a woman's speech and 15
  behaviour to his own desire, and make her believe she's
  the suitor herself, never give back till he has made her
  yield to it.
Fres. Indeed among our equals, madam, but otherwise we
  shall be put horribly out o' countenance.   20
Lev. Thou art deceived, Fresco. Ladies are as courteous
  as yeomen's wives, and methinks they should be more
  gentle. Hot diet and soft ease makes 'em, like wax always

---

177. *confident*] convincing.

II. v. o.1. manned] accompanied.
12–13. *a . . . purse*] Cf. Tilley, S759.

kept warm, more easy to take impression.—Prithee untie
my shoe.—What, art thou shamefaced too? Go roundly   25
to work, man. My leg is not gouty; 'twill endure the feeling, I warrant thee. Come hither, Fresco; thine ear.—
'S dainty, I mistook the place; I missed thine ear and hit
thy lip.

Fres. Your ladyship has made me blush.   30

Lev. That shows th' art full o' lusty blood and thou knowest
not how to use it. Let me see thy hand. Thou shouldst not
be shamefaced by thy hand, Fresco. Here's a brawny flesh
and a hairy skin, both signs of an able body. I do not like
these phlegmatic, smooth-skinned, soft-fleshed fellows.   35
They are like candied suckets when they begin to perish,
which I would always empty my closet of and give 'em
my chambermaid.—I have some skill in palmistry; by
this line that stands directly against me thou shouldst be
near a good fortune, Fresco, if thou hadst the grace to en-   40
tertain it.

Fres. O what is that, madam, I pray?

Lev. No less than the love of a fair lady, if thou dost not lose
her with faint-heartedness.

Fres. A lady, madam? Alas, a lady is a great thing; I cannot   45
compass her.

Lev. No? Why, I am a lady. Am I so great I cannot be compassed? Clasp my waist and try.

Fres. I could find i' my heart, madam.   SEBASTIAN *knocks within.*

Lev. 'Uds body, my husband! Faint-hearted fool, I think   50
thou wert begotten between the North Pole and the con-

---

28. *'S dainty*] By God's dignity.
36. *suckets*] succates or succades, fruit preserved in sugar. Cf. Middleton,
Women Beware Women (ed. Bullen), III. i. 269–70:
    Why, here's an old wench would trot into a bawd now
    For some dry sucket, or a colt in march-pane.
46. *compass*] obtain.
47–8. *compassed*] (*a*) attained, (*b*) encircled (in an embrace).
50. *'Uds*] God's.
51–2. *congealed passage*] probably the route to Japan and China by the
North Pole, discovered by Henry Hudson in 1607.

gealed passage. Now, like an ambitious coward that
betrays himself with fearful delay, you must suffer for the
treason you never committed. Go, hide thyself behind
yond' arras instantly.   FRESCO *hides himself.*   55

Enter SEBASTIAN.

Sebastian! What do you here so late?

Seb. Nothing yet, but I hope I shall.   *Kisses her.*

Lev. Y' are very bold.

Seb. And you very valiant, for you met me at full career.

Lev. You come to ha' me move your father's reconciliation.   60
I'll write a word or two i' your behalf.

Seb. A word or two, madam? That you do for me will not be
contained in less than the compass of two sheets. But in
plain terms, shall we take the opportunity of privateness?

Lev. What to do?   65

Seb. To dance the beginning of the world after the English
manner.

Lev. Why not after the French or Italian?

Seb. Fie, they dance it preposterously, backward.

Lev. Are you so active to dance?   70

Seb. I can shake my heels.

Lev. Y' are well made for 't.

Seb. Measure me from top to toe, you shall not find me differ
much from the true standard of proportion.

BELFOREST *knocks within.*

Lev. I think I am accursed, Sebastian. There's one at the door   75

52–3. *like . . . delay*] i.e., like a coward who wishes to overcome his
cowardice but finds excuses for inaction.

59. *full career*] in jousting, a charge at full speed.

60. *move*] urge.

63. *sheets*] (*a*) sheets of paper, (*b*) bed sheets.

66–7. *dance . . . manner*] i.e., have sexual intercourse. 'The beginning of
the world' was a popular dance tune, known also as 'Sellenger's Round'.
Cf. Heywood, *A Woman Killed with Kindness* (ed. Van Fossen), ii. 31–2,
47–8. The music is reproduced in W. Chappell, ed., *Old English Popular
Music*, rev. by H. E. Wooldridge (1893), I, 256–7.

69. *preposterously*] (*a*) ridiculously, (*b*) pervertedly.

has beaten opportunity away from us. In brief, I love
thee, and it shall not be long before I give thee a testimony
of it. To save thee now from suspicion, do no more but
draw thy rapier, chafe thyself, and when he comes in rush
by without taking notice of him. Only seem to be angry,   80
and let me alone for the rest.

Enter BELFOREST.

Seb. Now by the hand of Mercury—   *Exit.*
Bel. What's the matter, wife?
Lev. Ooh, ooh, husband!
Bel. Prithee what ail'st thou, woman?   85
Lev. O feel my pulse. It beats, I warrant you. Be patient a
   little, sweet husband; tarry but till my breath come to me
   again, and I'll satisfy you.
Bel. What ails Sebastian? He looks so distractedly.
Lev. The poor gentleman's almost out on 's wits, I think. You   90
   remember the displeasure his father took against him
   about the liberty of speech he used even now when your
   daughter went to be married?
Bel. Yes, what of that?
Lev. 'T has crazed him sure. He met a poor man i' the street   95
   even now. Upon what quarrel I know not, but he pursued
   him so violently that if my house had not been his rescue,
   he had surely killed him.
Bel. What a strange desperate young man is that!
Lev. Nay, husband, he grew so in rage when he saw the man   100
   was conveyed from him that he was ready even to have
   drawn his naked weapon upon me. And had not your
   knocking at the door prevented him, surely h' had done
   something to me.
Bel. Where's the man?   105

---

79. *chafe thyself*] i.e., make yourself angry.
102. *naked weapon*] (*a*) sword, (*b*) sexual organ.
103–4. *done something*] offered violence (with a covert suggestion of
sexual assault).

Lev. Alas, here. I warrant you the poor fearful soul is scarce
come to himself again yet. [*Aside*] If the fool have any
wit he will apprehend me. [*To* FRESCO] Do you hear, sir?
You may be bold to come forth; the Fury that haunted
you is gone.   110

                FRESCO *peeps fearfully forth from behind the arras.*

Fres. Are you sure he is gone?

Bel. He's gone, he's gone, I warrant thee.

Fres. I would I were gone too. Has shook me almost into a
dead palsy.

Bel. How fell the difference between you?   115

Fres. I would I were out at the back door.

Bel. Th' art safe enough. Prithee tell 's the falling out.

Fres. Yes sir, when I have recovered my spirits. My memory
is almost frighted from me.—O, so, so, so.—Why, sir, as
I came along the street, sir,—this same gentleman came   120
stumbling after me and trod o' my heel.—I cried O. Do
you cry, sirrah? says he. Let me see your heel; if it be not
hurt, I'll make you cry for something. So he claps my
head between his legs and pulls off my shoe. I having
shifted no socks in a sennight, the gentleman cried Foh,   125
and said my feet were base and cowardly feet; they
stunk for fear. Then he knocked my shoe about my pate,
and I cried O, once more. In the meantime comes a
shag-haired dog by and rubs against his shins. The
gentleman took the dog in shag-hair to be some watch-   130
man in a rug gown, and swore he would hang me up at
the next door with my lantern in my hand, that passen-
gers might see their way as they went without rubbing

---

108. *apprehend*] understand.

125. *sennight*] week.

129. *shag-haired*] having long, rough, matted hair (*O.E.D.*).

131. *rug gown*] a coat of rough woollen material, a sort of coarse frieze in
common use in the seventeenth century (*O.E.D.*). It was regarded as the
usual dress of students, magicians, astrologers, etc., when engaged in their
speculations. Cf. Marston, *What You Will* (ed. Bullen), IV. i. 179–80:
    Lamp-oil, watch-candles, rug-gowns, and small juice,
    Thin commons, four o'clock rising,—I renounce you all.

against gentlemen's shins. So, for want of a cord, he
took his own garters off, and as he was going to make a   135
noose, I watched my time and ran away. And as I ran,
indeed, I bid him hang himself in his own garters. So he,
in choler, pursued me hither as you see.

Bel. Why this savours of distraction.

Lev. Of mere distraction.   140

Fres. [*Aside*] Howsoever it savours, I am sure it smells like a
lie.

Bel. Thou may'st go forth at the back door, honest fellow; the
way is private and safe.

Fres. So it had need, for your fore-door here is both common   145
and dangerous.   *Exit* BELFOREST.

Lev. Good night, honest Fresco.

Fres. Good night, madam. If you get me kissing o' ladies
again—   *Exit.*

Lev. This falls out handsomely.   150
But yet the matter does not well succeed
Till I have brought it to the very deed.   *Exit.*

[II. vi]

Enter CHARLEMONT, *in arms, a* Musketeer, *and a* Sergeant.

Char. Sergeant, what hour o' the night is 't?

Ser. About one.

Char. I would you would relieve me, for I am

---

137. *hang . . . garters*] a common expression; cf. Tilley, G42; Shakespeare, *1 Henry IV*, II. ii. 49–50:
> Go, hang thyself in thine own heir apparent garters.

139. *savours*] smells.

140. *mere*] pure, unmixed (*O.E.D.*).

145. *fore-door*] (*a*) front door of house, (*b*) genitals.

common] for general use, as of a whore. Cf. 'Singing Simpkin', in C. R.
Baskervill, *The Elizabethan Jig* (Chicago, 1923), p. 446:
> *Wife.* I have a place behind here,
>   Which yet is known to no man.
> *Simp.* She has a place before too,
>   But that is all to common.

So heavy that I shall ha' much ado
To stand out my perdu.   *Thunder and lightning.*

Ser.   I'll e'en but walk   5
The round, sir, and then presently return.

Musk. For God's sake, sergeant, relieve me. Above five hours
together in so foul a stormy night as this!

Ser. Why 'tis a music, soldier. Heaven and earth are now in
consort, when the thunder and the cannon play to one   10
another.   *Exit.*

Char. I know not why I should be thus inclin'd
To sleep. I feel my disposition press'd
With a necessity of heaviness.
Soldier! If thou hast any better eyes,   15
I prithee wake me when the sergeant comes.

Musk. Sir, 'tis so dark and stormy that I shall
Scarce either see or hear him ere he comes
Upon me.

Char.   I cannot force myself to wake.   *Sleeps.*

Enter the GHOST OF MONTFERRERS.

Mont. Return to France, for thy old father's dead   20

7. *Musk.*] *This ed.; Soul. Q (and throughout scene).*

---

4. *heavy*] i.e., with sleep.
5. *perdu*] sentinel perdue, a very dangerous outpost duty (Nicoll). Cf. Shakespeare, *King Lear*, IV. vii. 35–6:
          . . . to watch—poor perdu!—
          With this thin helm?
9–10. *in consort*] (*a*) in fellowship, (*b*) performing together as musicians. Cf. Shakespeare, *Romeo and Juliet*, III. i. 50–2:
     Consort! What! dost thou make us minstrels? an thou make minstrels of us, look to hear nothing but discords.
10. *play to*] sound in harmony with.
13. *press'd*] assailed.
14. *necessity*] compulsion.
19. *wake*] stay awake.
19.1. *GHOST*] Miss L. B. Campbell has pointed out that the ghost of Montferrers is the least Senecan, most Christian ghost in all Elizabethan tragedy. See 'Theories of Revenge in Elizabethan England', *M.P.*, XXVIII (1930–1), 296. Cf. also R. H. West, *The Invisible World* (Athens, Ga., 1939), p. 187.

And thou by murder disinherited.
Attend with patience the success of things,
But leave revenge unto the King of kings.   *Exit.*

                                        CHARLEMONT *starts and wakes.*

Char. O my affrighted soul, what fearful dream
  Was this that wak'd me ? Dreams are but the rais'd   25
  Impressions of premeditated things,
  By serious apprehension left upon
  Our minds, or else th' imaginary shapes
  Of objects proper to th' complexion or

---

22. *patience*] The word is used in the religious sense of uncomplaining acceptance of fate as a manifestation of divine will, coupled with faith and hope in a future felicity promised by Christ. This latter element differentiates it from classical stoicism, with its indifference both to pleasure and to pain.

 success] result.

25–30. *Dreams . . . bodies*] Collins calls attention to Thomas Lodge's explanation of dreams in *A Fig for Momus* (1595). Cf. in particular [Sig. E4^r]:

> Dreames then (in sleep our spirits true retreate)
> Do challenge their predominance and seate:
> And in their natures, are but fantasies
> Made by the motion of imageries,
> According to the sleeper's habitude
> Of euery sensible similitude.
> So then, all dreames from diuers causes grow,
> And from th' interior, or th' exterior flow:
> Th' interior likewise hath a double right,
> The one is mental, clayming by the spright,
> Where through in sleep (the fantasie and thought
> Encountring) strange and rare effects are wrought:
> Resembling those, which our affections kept,
> And thoughts did trauel on before we slept:
> The other cause takes his fruition,
> And being from the bodies disposition.

Collins calls attention to Clermont's attempt scientifically to explain dreams in Chapman's *Revenge of Bussy D'Ambois*, v. i.

 27. *apprehension*] grasping with the intellect.

 29. *complexion*] in medieval physiology, the combination of the humours of the body in a certain proportion. Cf. Thomas Elyot, *The Castel of Helthe* (1539) [Sig. A2^r]:

> Complexion is a combynation of two dyuers qualities of the foure elementes in one bodye, as hotte and drye of the fyre: hotte and moyste of the Ayre, colde and moyste of the water, colde and dry of the Erth. But although all these complexions be assembled in euery body of man and

The dispositions of our bodies. These   30
Can neither of them be the cause why I
Should dream thus, for my mind has not been mov'd
With any one conception of a thought
To such a purpose, nor my nature wont
To trouble me with fantasies of terror.   35
It must be something that my Genius would
Inform me of. Now gracious heaven forbid!
O, let my spirit be depriv'd of all
Foresight and knowledge ere it understand
That vision acted, or divine that act   40
To come. Why should I think so? Left I not
My worthy father i' the kind regard
Of a most loving uncle? Soldier, saw'st
No apparition of a man?

Musk.   You dream,
Sir; I saw nothing.

Char.   Tush, these idle dreams   45
Are fabulous. Our boiling fantasies
Like troubled waters falsify the shapes
Of things retain'd in them, and make 'em seem
Confounded when they are distinguish'd. So
My actions daily conversant with war,   50
The argument of blood and death, had left,
Perhaps, th' imaginary presence of
Some bloody accident upon my mind,

---

woman, yet the body taketh his denomination of those qualities, whyche
abounde in hym, more thanne in the other, as hereafter inseweth.
36. *Genius*] tutelary power.
40. *That vision acted*] i.e., that what I have beheld represents something
which has actually occurred.
42. *regard*] care or protection (*O.E.D.*).
46. *fabulous*] untrue.
49. *Confounded*] mixed together. Cf. Marlowe, *Doctor Faustus* (ed.
Jump), iii. 61–2:
          This word 'damnation' terrifies not him,
          For he confounds hell in Elysium.
distinguish'd] separate.

Which, mix'd confusedly with other thoughts,
Whereof th' remembrance of my father might   55
Be one, presented all together seem
Incorporate, as if his body were
The owner of that blood, the subject of
That death, when he's at Paris and that blood
Shed here. It may be thus. I would not leave   60
The war, for reputation's sake, upon
An idle apprehension, a vain dream.

Enter the GHOST.

Musk. Stand, stand, I say. No? Why then have at thee.
Sir, if you will not stand, I'll make you fall.
Nor stand, nor fall? Nay, then the Devil's dam   65
Has broke her husband's head, for sure it is a spirit.
I shot it through, and yet it will not fall.   *Exit.*

The GHOST *approaches* CHARLEMONT.
He fearfully avoids it.

Char. O pardon me. My doubtful heart was slow
To credit that which I did fear to know.   *Exeunt.*

---

57. *Incorporate*] combined and endowed with a body.
68. *doubtful*] (*a*) doubting, (*b*) fearful.

Act III

[III. i]

Enter [D'AMVILLE *with*] *the funeral of* MONTFERRERS.

D'Am. Set down the body. Pay earth what she lent,
But she shall bear a living monument
To let succeeding ages truly know
That she is satisfy'd what he did owe,
Both principal and use, because his worth   5
Was better at his death than at his birth.

A dead march. Enter the funeral of CHARLEMONT *as
a soldier.*

And with his body place that memory
Of noble Charlemont, his worthy son,
And give their graves the rites that do belong
To soldiers. They were soldiers both. The father   10
Held open war with sin, the son with blood;
This in a war more gallant, that more good.

                                                  The first volley.

There place their arms, and here their epitaphs,
And may these lines survive the last of graves:

Act III] Actus tertij Scena prima *Q.*   0.1. D'AMVILLE *with*] *This ed.*
7. And] *D'am.* And *Q.*   13. There] *D'am.* There *Q.*

---

2. *living monument*] Cf. Shakespeare, *Hamlet*, v. i. 319:
        This grave shall have a living monument.
4. *satisfy'd what*] satisfied in respect of what.
5. *use*] interest. Cf. 1. ii. 146.
7. *memory*] i.e., either a body which has been obtained to represent
Charlemont's remains (cf. l. 25) or some substitute for a body.

[*Reads*]

The Epitaph of MONTFERRERS.

Here lie the ashes of that earth and fire   15
  Whose heat and fruit did feed and warm the poor,
And they, as if they would in sighs expire
  And into tears dissolve, his death deplore.
He did that good freely, for goodness' sake,
  Unforc'd, for gen'rousness he held so dear   20
That he fear'd none but him that did him make,
  And yet he serv'd him more for love than fear.
So's life provided that though he did die
A sudden death, yet died not suddenly.

The Epitaph of CHARLEMONT.

His body lies interr'd within this mould,   25
Who died a young man, yet departed old,
And in all strength of youth that man can have
Was ready still to drop into his grave.
For ag'd in virtue, with a youthful eye
He welcom'd it, being still prepar'd to die;   30
And living so, though young depriv'd of breath,
He did not suffer an untimely death,
But we may say of his brave bless'd decease:
He died in war, and yet he died in peace.

                                            The second volley.

O might that fire revive the ashes of   35
This phoenix! Yet the wonder would not be
So great as he was good and wond'red at
For that. His life's example was so true
A practique of religion's theory

14.1. *Reads*] Symonds.   35. O] *D'am.* O *Q.*

---

24. suddenly] without preparation.
30. still] always.
36. *phoenix*] the legendary bird constantly reborn out of its own ashes, a conventional symbol for immortality.
39. *practique*] practice.

That her divinity seem'd rather the   40
Description than th' instruction of his life.
And of his goodness was his virtuous son
A worthy imitator. So that on
These two Herculean pillars where their arms
Are plac'd there may be writ *Non ultra*. For   45
Beyond their lives, as well for youth as age,
Nor young nor old, in merit or in name,
Shall e'er exceed their virtues or their fame.
                                        The third volley.
'Tis done. Thus fair accompliments make foul
Deeds gracious. Charlemont, come now when t' wou't,   50
I've bury'd under these two marble stones
Thy living hopes and thy dead father's bones.   *Exeunt.*

Enter CASTABELLA *mourning, to the monument of* CHARLEMONT.

Cast. O thou that know'st me justly Charlemont's,
Though in the forc'd possession of another,
Since from thine own free spirit we receive it   55
That our affections cannot be compell'd
Though our actions may, be not displeas'd if on
The altar of his tomb I sacrifice
My tears. They are the jewels of my love
Dissolved into grief, and fall upon   60
His blasted spring as April dew upon
A sweet young blossom shak'd before the time.

50. t' wou't] *This ed.;* t'wut *Q;* th'wilt *Collins;* thou wilt *Symonds.*

44–5. *Herculean . . . ultra*] i.e., the funeral monuments, bearing the coats
of arms of the dead men, are likened to the pillars set up by Hercules at
the Straits of Gibraltar, forbidding further penetration of the seas.

45. Non ultra] no further.

47. *name*] reputation.

49. *accompliments*] gracious words. Cf. I. ii. 60.

50. *t' wou't*] thou wilt. Cf. II. ii. 4.

58–9. *altar . . . tears*] Cf. Shakespeare, *Two Gentlemen of Verona*, III. ii.
73–4:

        Say that upon the altar of her beauty
        You sacrifice your tears, your sighs, your heart.

Enter CHARLEMONT *with a* Servant.

Char. Go see my trunks dispos'd of. I'll but walk
       A turn or two i' th' church and follow you.   *Exit* Servant.
       O, here's the fatal monument of my   65
       Dead father first presented to mine eye.
       What's here ? In memory of Charlemont ?
       Some false relation has abus'd belief.
       I am deluded. But I thank thee, Heaven.
       For ever let me be deluded thus.   70
       My Castabella mourning o'er my hearse ?
       Sweet Castabella, rise; I am not dead.
Cast. O Heaven defend me!   *Falls in a swoon.*
Char.   I beshrew my rash
       And inconsid'rate passion.—Castabella!—
       That could not think—my Castabella!—that   75
       My sudden presence might affright her sense.
       I prithee, my affection, pardon me.   *She rises.*
       Reduce thy understanding to thine eye.
       Within this habit which thy misinform'd
       Conceit takes only for a shape live both   80
       The soul and body of thy Charlemont.
Cast. I feel a substance warm and soft and moist,
       Subject to the capacity of sense.
Char. Which spirits are not, for their essence is
       Above the nature and the order of   85
       Those elements whereof our senses are
       Created. Touch my lip. Why turn'st thou from me ?
Cast. Grief above griefs! That which should woe relieve,
       Wish'd and obtain'd, gives greater cause to grieve.
Char. Can Castabella think it cause of grief   90

---

64. *church*] i.e., churchyard.
68. *relation*] tale.
77. *my affection*] my love (the vocative is unusual).
80. *Conceit*] imagination.
    shape] phantom, illusion. Cf. Shakespeare, *Two Gentlemen of Verona*, IV.
ii. 133:
                To worship shadows and adore false shapes.

           That the relation of my death proves false ?

Cast. The presence of the person we affect,
      Being hopeless to enjoy him, makes our grief
      More passionate than if we saw him not.

Char. Why not enjoy ? Has absence chang'd thee ?

Cast.   Yes,   95
      From maid to wife.

Char.   Art marry'd ?

Cast.   O, I am.

Char. Marry'd! Had not my mother been a woman,
      I should protest against the chastity
      Of all thy sex. How can the merchant or
      The mariner, absent whole years, from wives   100
      Experienc'd in the satisfaction of
      Desire, promise themselves to find their sheets
      Unspotted with adultery at their
      Return, when you that never had the sense
      Of actual temptation could not stay   105
      A few short months ?

Cast.   O, do but hear me speak.

Char. But thou wert wise and didst consider that
      A soldier might be maim'd and so perhaps
      Lose his ability to please thee.

Cast.   No.
      That weakness pleases me in him I have.   110

Char. What, marry'd to a man unable too ?
      O strange incontinence! Why, was thy blood
      Increas'd to such a pleurisy of lust
      That of necessity there must a vein
      Be open'd, though by one that had no skill   115
      To do 't ?

97. Marry'd!] Married ? *Q.*

---

  92. *affect*] love.

  97–9. *Marry'd . . . sex*] The recollection of *Hamlet* seems very clear. Cf.
I. ii. 129–59, III. i. 141–58.

  113. *pleurisy*] superabundance (*O.E.D.*).

| *Cast.* | Sir, I beseech you hear me. |
| *Char.* | Speak. |

Cast. Heav'n knows I am unguilty of this act.

Char. Why, wert thou forc'd to do 't?

Cast.   Heav'n knows I was.

Char. What villain did it?

Cast.   Your uncle D'Amville.

And he that dispossess'd my love of you   120
Hath disinherited you of possession.

Char. Disinherited? Wherein have I deserv'd
To be depriv'd of my dear father's love?

Cast. Both of his love and him. His soul's at rest,
But here your injur'd patience may behold   125
The signs of his lamented memory.

                    CHARLEMONT *finds his father's monument.*

H' has found it. When I took him for a ghost
I could endure the torment of my fear
More eas'ly than I can his sorrows hear.   *Exit.*

Char. Of all men's griefs must mine be singular?   130
Without example? Here I met my grave,
And all men's woes are bury'd i' their graves
But mine. In mine my miseries are born.
I prithee, sorrow, leave a little room
In my confounded and tormented mind   135
For understanding to deliberate
The cause or author of this accident—
A close advantage of my absence made
To dispossess me both of land and wife,
And all the profit does arise to him   140
By whom my absence was first mov'd and urg'd.
These circumstances, uncle, tell me you

118. Why,] Why? *Q.*

---

121. *disinherited . . . possession*] i.e., taken possession of your father's
property.

125. *patience*] Cf. II. vi. 22.

130. *singular*] unique.

138. *close*] secret.

I

Are the suspected author of those wrongs,
Whereof the lightest is more heavy than
The strongest patience can endure to bear.   *Exit.*   145

[III. ii]

Enter D'AMVILLE, SEBASTIAN, *and* LANGUEBEAU [SNUFFE].

D'Am. Now sir, your business ?
Seb.   My annuity.
D'Am. Not a denier.
Seb.   How would you ha' me live ?
D'Am. Why, turn crier. Cannot you turn crier ?
Seb. Yes.
D'Am.   Then do so; y' have a good voice for 't.
    Y' are excellent at crying of a rape.   5
Seb. Sir, I confess in particular respect to yourself I was some-
    what forgetful. Gen'ral honesty possessed me.
D'Am. Go, th' art the base corruption of my blood,
    And like a tetter grow'st unto my flesh.
Seb. Inflict any punishment upon me. The severity shall not   10
    discourage me if it be not shameful, so you'll but put
    money i' my purse. The want of money makes a free spirit
    more mad than the possession does an usurer.
D'Am. Not a farthing.
Seb. Would you ha' me turn purse-taker ? 'Tis the next way to   15
    do 't. For want is like the rack; it draws a man to endanger
    himself to the gallows rather than endure it.

III. ii. 9. grow'st] growes't Q.

III. ii. 2. *denier*] a French coin, equal to one-twelfth of a sou, originally of
silver, but from the sixteenth century on of copper and of very little value.
    8–9. *Go . . . flesh*] Cf. Shakespeare, *King Lear*, II. iv. 224–6:
> But yet thou art my flesh, my blood, my daughter;
> Or rather a disease that's in my flesh,
> Which I must needs call mine.
    9. *tetter*] any skin disease.
    11–12. *put . . . purse*] Cf. Shakespeare, *Othello*, I. iii. 345–7:
    Put money in thy purse; follow these wars; defeat thy favour with a
usurped beard; I say, put money in thy purse.

Enter CHARLEMONT; D'AMVILLE *counterfeits to take him
for a ghost.*

D'Am. What art thou? Stay! Assist my troubled sense.
My apprehension will distract me. Stay!

LANGUEBEAU SNUFFE *avoids him fearfully.*

Seb. What art thou? Speak!
Char.　　　　　　　　The spirit of Charlemont.　　20
D'Am. O stay. Compose me. I dissolve.
Lang. No, 'tis profane. Spirits are invisible. 'Tis the fiend i'
　　the likeness of Charlemont. I will have no conversation
　　with Satan.　　　　　　　　　　　　　　*Exit.*
Seb. The spirit of Charlemont? I'll try that.　　25
　　　　　　　　Strike[s], and the blow [is] returned.
　　'Fore God, thou sayest true; th' art all spirit.
D'Am. Go call the officers.　　　　　　　　*Exit.*
Char. Th' art a villain and the son of a villain.
Seb. You lie.　　　　　　*[They] fight.* SEBASTIAN *is down.*
Char. Have at thee.　　　　　　　　　　30

Enter the GHOST OF MONTFERRERS.

　　Revenge, to thee I'll dedicate this work.
Mont. Hold, Charlemont!
　　Let him revenge my murder and thy wrongs
　　To whom the justice of revenge belongs.　　*Exit.*
Char. You torture me between the passion of　　35
　　My blood and the religion of my soul.

　　　　　　　　　　　　SEBASTIAN *rises.*
Seb. A good honest fellow.

---

19. *apprehension*] perception.
distract] make mad.
19.1. him] i.e., Charlemont.
21. *Compose*] calm.
22–4. *No . . . Satan*] This was a common view of ghosts, although Catho-
lics could regard them as souls in purgatory. Cf. Shakespeare, *Hamlet*, I.
v. 9–13. See R. H. West, *The Invisible World*, pp. 181–5.
26. *spirit*] (*a*) ghost, (*b*) vigour.

Enter D'AMVILLE *with* Officers.

D'Am. What, wounded ? Apprehend him. Sir, is this
        Your salutation for the courtesy
        I did you when we parted last ? You ha'   40
        Forgot I lent you a thousand crowns. [*To the* Officers] First let
        Him answer for this riot. When the law
        Is satisfy'd for that, an action for
        His debt shall clap him up again. [*To* CHARLEMONT] I took
        You for a spirit, and I'll conjure you   45
        Before I ha' done.

Char.   No, I'll turn conjurer. Devil!
        Within this circle, in the midst of all
        Thy force and malice, I conjure thee do
        Thy worst.

D'Am.   Away with him!

                                Exeunt Officers *with* CHARLEMONT.

Seb.   Sir, I have got
        A scratch or two here for your sake. I hope   50
        You'll give me money to pay the surgeon.

D'Am. Borachio, fetch me a thousand crowns. I am
        Content to countenance the freedom of
        Your spirit when 'tis worthily employed.
        A' God's name, give behaviour the full scope   55
        Of gen'rous liberty, but let it not
        Disperse and spend itself in courses of

---

43. *action*] lawsuit.

47. *circle*] The importance of the circle in the art of conjuring is explained
by Cornelius Agrippa in his *Three Books of Occult Philosophy*, tr. by J. F.
(1651):

    . . . Of these first of all a Circle doth answer to Unity, and the number
    ten; for unity is the Center, and the circumference of all things; and the
    number ten being heaped together returns into a unity from whence it
    had its beginning, being the end of all numbers . . hence a circle being
    the largest and perfectest of all [geometrical figures] is judged to be the
    most fit for bindings and conjurations; Whence they who abjure evil
    spirits, are wont to environ themselves about with a circle. (Cited by
    West, *The Invisible World*, p. 126.)

53. *countenance*] support.

Unbounded licence. Here, pay for your hurts.   *Exit.*

Seb. I thank you, sir. Gen'rous liberty—that is to say, freely
to bestow my abilities to honest purposes. Methinks I   60
should not follow that instruction now, if having the
means to do an honest office for an honest fellow, I should
neglect it. Charlemont lies in prison for a thousand
crowns, and here I have a thousand crowns. Honesty tells
me 'twere well done to release Charlemont. But discretion   65
says I had much ado to come by this, and when this shall
be gone I know not where to finger any more, especially if
I employ it to this use, which is like to endanger me into
my father's perpetual displeasure. And then I may go
hang myself, or be forced to do that will make another   70
save me the labour. No matter. Charlemont, thou gav'st
me my life, and that's somewhat of a purer earth than
gold, as fine as it is. 'Tis no courtesy I do thee, but thank-
fulness. I owe thee it and I'll pay it. He fought bravely,
but the officers dragged him villainously. Arrant knaves,   75
for using him so discourteously, may the sins o' the poor
people be so few that you sha' not be able to spare so much
out o' your gettings as will pay for the hire of a lame
starved hackney to ride to an execution, but go a-foot to
the gallows and be hanged. May elder brothers turn good   80
husbands and younger brothers get good wives, that there
be no need of debt-books nor use of sergeants. May there
be all peace but i' the war and all charity but i' the devil,
so that prisons may be turned to hospitals, though the
officers live o' the benevolence. If this curse might come   85
to pass, the world would say, *Blessed be he that curseth.* *Exit.*

---

81. wives] *Q (corrected); * wits *Q (uncorrected).*

---

81. *husbands*] (*a*) men careful with property, (*b*) married men.
82. *sergeants*] sheriffs' officers, employed usually to make arrests for debt.
85. *benevolence*] alms.

[III. iii]

Enter CHARLEMONT *in prison.*

shallow
theist who expects
rational justice

Char. I grant thee, Heaven, thy goodness doth command
          Our punishments, but yet no further than
          The measure of our sins. How should they else
          Be just ? Or how should that good purpose of
          Thy justice take effect by bounding men   5
          Within the confines of humanity,
          When our afflictions do exceed our crimes ?
          Then they do rather teach the barb'rous world
          Examples that extend her cruelties
          Beyond their own dimensions, and instruct   10
          Our actions to be more, more barbarous.
          O my afflicted soul, how torment swells
          Thy apprehension with profane conceit
          Against the sacred justice of my God!
          Our own constructions are the authors of   15
          Our misery. We never measure our
          Conditions but with men above us in
          Estate, so while our spirits labour to
          Be higher than our fortunes, th' are more base.
          Since all those attributes which make men seem   20
          Superior to us are man's subjects and
          Were made to serve him, the repining man
          Is of a servile spirit to deject

III. iii. 11. more, more] *Q, Nicoll;* much more *Collins.*   22. him, the]
him. The *Q.*

III. iii. 3. *they*] i.e., punishments.
    4–7. *Or how . . . crimes*] i.e., how can your benevolent justice impose upon
us the limitations incident to humanity when our sufferings are greater
than we deserve ?
    11. *more, more*] There seems little warrant for Collins's emendation, since
intensification by repetition is quite common.
    13. *apprehension*] understanding.
    conceit] fancy.
    15. *constructions*] ways of interpreting.

The value of himself below their estimation.

Enter SEBASTIAN *with the* Keeper.

Seb. Here, take my sword.—How now, my wild swagg'rer,   25
        y' are tame enough now, are you not? The penury of a
        prison is like a soft consumption. 'Twill humble the pride
        o' your mortality and arm your soul in complete patience
        to endure the weight of affliction without feeling it. What,
        hast no music in thee? Th' hast trebles and basses   30
        enough, treble injury and base usage. But trebles and
        basses make poor music without means. Thou want'st
        means, dost? What, dost droop? Art dejected?
Char. No, sir. I have a heart above the reach
        Of thy most violent maliciousness,   35
        A fortitude in scorn of thy contempt—
        Since Fate is pleas'd to have me suffer it—
        That can bear more than thou hast power t' inflict.
        I was a baron; that thy father has
        Depriv'd me of. Instead of that I am   40
        Created king. I've lost a signory
        That was confin'd within a piece of earth,
        A wart upon the body of the world.
        But now I am an emp'ror of a world,
        This little world of man. My passions are   45

---

24. *their estimation*] i.e., the value assigned to men who seem superior
to us.

27. *soft*] easily endured.

consumption] wasting of the body by disease.

31–3. *trebles . . . means*] Collins calls attention to the same play on words
in John Lyly's *Gallathea* (1592) [Sig. H1ᵛ]:

> *Venus* Can you sing?
> *Rafe* Baselie.
> *Venus* And you?
> *Dick* Meanely.
> *Venus* And what can you doe?
> *Robin* If they duble it, I will treble it.

The 'mean' in harmony is the middle or intermediate part.

41. *signory*] lordship.

45. *little . . . man*] Cf. Shakespeare, *Richard II*, III. ii. 153–4:

My subjects, and I can command them laugh,
Whilst thou dost tickle 'em to death with misery.

Seb. 'Tis bravely spoken, and I love thee for 't. Thou liest
here for a thousand crowns. Here are a thousand to redeem thee—not for the ransom o' my life thou gav'st me;   50
that I value not at one crown. 'Tis none o' my deed; thank
my father for 't. 'Tis his goodness. Yet he looks not for
thanks, for he does it underhand, out of a reserved disposition to do thee good without ostentation.—Out o' great
heart you'll refuse 't now, will you?   55

Char. No. Since I must submit myself to Fate,
I never will neglect the offer of
One benefit, but entertain them as
Her favours and th' inductions to some end
Of better fortune, as whose instrument   60
I thank thy courtesy.

Seb.   Well, come along.   *Exeunt.*

[III. iv]

Enter D'AMVILLE *and* CASTABELLA.

D'Am. Daughter, you do not well to urge me. I
Ha' done no more than justice. Charlemont
Shall die and rot in prison, and 'tis just.

Cast. O father, mercy is an attribute

And that small model of the barren earth
Which serves as paste and cover to our bones.
Macbeth, I. iii. 140:
                    my single state of man.
This comparison of the human body to either a kingdom or the physical
earth is an Elizabethan commonplace, closely related to a conception of the
universe as an ordered and unified creation in which man, the state, and the
earth itself occupied parallel positions in the divine scheme. Cf. E. M. W.
Tillyard, *The Elizabethan World Picture* (London, 1945).

    53. *reserved*] secret or hidden.
    59. *inductions*] preliminaries.

    III. iv. 4–12. *O . . . weakness*] Cf. Shakespeare, *Merchant of Venice,* IV. i.
198–202:
                    Though justice be thy plea, consider this,

As high as justice, an essential part   5
Of his unbounded goodness, whose divine
Impression, form, and image man should bear.
And methinks man should love to imitate
His mercy, since the only countenance
Of justice were destruction, if the sweet   10
And loving favour of his mercy did
Not mediate between it and our weakness.

D'Am. Forbear. You will displease me. He shall rot.

Cast. Dear sir, since by your greatness you
Are nearer heav'n in place, be nearer it   15
In goodness. Rich men should transcend the poor
As clouds the earth, rais'd by the comfort of
The sun to water dry and barren grounds.
If neither the impression in your soul
Of goodness, nor the duty of your place   20
As goodness' substitute can move you, then
Let Nature, which in savages, in beasts,
Can stir to pity, tell you that he is
Your kinsman.

D'Am.   You expose your honesty
To strange construction. Why should you so urge   25
Release for Charlemont ? Come, you profess

That in the course of justice none of us
Should see salvation: we do pray for mercy,
And that same prayer doth teach us all to render
The deeds of mercy.

Measure for Measure, II. ii. 73–9:
Why, all the souls that were were forfeit once;
And He that might the vantage best have took,
Found out the remedy. How would you be,
If He, which is the top of judgment, should
But judge you as you are ? O! think on that,
And mercy then will breathe within your lips,
Like man new made.

9. *countenance*] manifestation.
20–1. *place . . . substitute*] i.e., position as a magistrate.
24. *honesty*] chastity.
25. *construction*] interpretation.

   More nearness to him than your modesty
   Can answer. You have tempted my suspicion.
   I tell thee he shall starve, and die, and rot.

     Enter CHARLEMONT *and* SEBASTIAN.

Char. Uncle, I thank you.
D'Am.   Much good do it you.   30
   Who did release him?
Seb.   I.   *Exit* CASTABELLA.
D'Am.   You are a villain.
Seb. Y' are my father.   *Exit*.
D'Am. [*Aside*]   I must temporize.
   [*To* CHARLEMONT] Nephew, had not his open freedom made
   My disposition known, I would ha' borne
   The course and inclination of my love   35
   According to the motion of the sun,
   Invisibly enjoy'd and understood.
Char. That shows your good works are directed to
   No other end than goodness. I was rash,
   I must confess, but—
D'Am.   I will excuse you.   40
   To lose a father and, as you may think,
   Be disinherited, it must be granted,
   Are motives to impatience. But for death,
   Who can avoid it? And for his estate,
   In the uncertainty of both your lives   45
   'Twas done discreetly to confer 't upon
   A known successor, being the next in blood,
   And one, dear nephew, whom in time to come
   You shall have cause to thank. I will not be
   Your dispossessor, but your guardian.   50
   I will supply your father's vacant place,
   To guide your green improvidence of youth

32. *Aside*] Collins.

---

33. *open freedom*] extreme frankness.
36. *According to*] like.

And make you ripe for your inheritance.

Char. Sir, I embrace your gen'rous promises.   [*They embrace.*]

Enter ROUSARD *sick, and* CASTABELLA.

Rous. Embracing? I behold the object that   55
    Mine eye affects. Dear cousin Charlemont!

D'Am. My elder son. He meets you happily,
    For with the hand of our whole family
    We interchange th' indenture of our loves.

Char. And I accept it, yet not joyfully   60
    Because y' are sick

D'Am.   Sir, his affection's sound
    Though he be sick in body.

Rous.   Sick indeed.
    A gen'ral weakness did surprise my health
    The very day I marry'd Castabella,
    As if my sickness were a punishment   65
    That did arrest me for some injury
    I then committed. [*To* CASTABELLA] Credit me, my love,
    I pity thy ill fortune to be match'd
    With such a weak unpleasing bedfellow.

Cast. Believe me, sir, it never troubles me.   70
    I am as much respectless to enjoy
    Such pleasure as ignorant what it is.

Char. Thy sex's wonder. Unhappy Charlemont.

D'Am. Come, let's to supper. There we will confirm
    The eternal bond of our concluded love.   *Exeunt.*

---

72. as] *Q;* as [Ime] *Nicoll.*

56. *affects*] loves.
59. *indenture*] formal declaration.
71. *respectless*] indifferent.
75. *concluded*] proven or demonstrated.

Act IV

Enter CATAPLASMA *and* SOQUETTE *with needlework.*

Cata. Come, Soquette, your work; let's examine your work.
What's here? A medlar with a plum tree growing hard by
it, the leaves o' the plum tree falling off, the gum issuing
out o' the perished joints, and the branches some of 'em
dead and some rotten, and yet but a young plum tree. In   5
good sooth, very pretty.

Soq. The plum tree, forsooth, grows so near the medlar that
the medlar sucks and draws all the sap from it and the
natural strength o' the ground, so that it cannot prosper.

Cata. How conceited you are! But here th' hast made a tree to   10
bear no fruit. Why's that?

Soq. There grows a savin tree next it, forsooth.

Cata. Forsooth, you are a little too witty in that.

Enter SEBASTIAN.

Act IV] Actus quarti Scena prima *Q*.

0.1. needlework] a conventional Elizabethan stage device to indicate
domestic scenes. Cf. Shakespeare, *Coriolanus*, I. iii.

2. *medlar*] The pear produced by this tree, *Mespilus Germania*, was, probably because of its shape, often used to refer to the female genital area, and
thus the word was used commonly with sexual significance. Cf. Shakespeare, *Romeo and Juliet*, II. i. 34–6:

> Now will he sit under a medlar tree,
> And wish his mistress were that kind of fruit
> As maids call medlars, when they laugh alone.

plum tree] used sometimes in an obscene sense. Cf. Nashe, *Have With
You to Saffron-Walden* (ed. McKerrow, rev. Wilson), III, 113:

> Yea, Madam *Gabriela*, are you such an old ierker? then Hey ding a ding,
> vp with your petticoats, haue at your plum-tree.

10. *conceited*] witty or facetious.

12. *savin tree*] a small bushy evergreen, *Juniperus Sabina*, whose dried
tops and berries, because they were strongly poisonous, were widely used
to induce abortions.

Seb. [*Embracing her*] But this honeysuckle winds about this
  whitethorn very prettily and lovingly, sweet Mistress   15
  Cataplasma.

Cata. Monsieur Sebastian! In good sooth, very uprightly
  welcome this evening.

Seb. What, moralizing upon this gentlewoman's needlework?
  Let's see.   20

Cata. No, sir, only examining whether it be done to the true
  nature and life o' the thing.

Seb. Here y' have set a medlar with a bachelor's button o' one
  side and a snail o' th' t'other. The bachelor's button should
  have held his head up more pertly towards the medlar;   25
  the snail o' th' t'other side should ha' been wrought with
  an artificial laziness, doubling his tail and putting out his
  horn but half the length, and then the medlar falling, as it
  were, from the lazy snail and inclining towards the pert
  bachelor's button, their branches spreading and winding   30
  one within another as if they did embrace. But here's a
  moral. A pop'ring pear tree growing upon the bank of a
  river, seeming continually to look downwards into the
  water as if it were enamoured of it, and ever as the fruit
  ripens lets it fall for love, as it were, into her lap; which   35
  the wanton stream, like a strumpet, no sooner receives
  but she carries it away and bestows it upon some other

---

14. *honeysuckle*] plant traditionally symbolic of love.

15. *whitethorn*] as one of the earliest plants to bloom in the springtime,
traditionally associated with love and dalliance.

17. *uprightly*] used with a sexual *double entendre*.

23. *bachelor's button*] a double button-like flower, *Ranunculus acontifolius*,
carried often by lovers in the belief that if the flower remained fresh their
love affairs would prosper. It was a conventional form in Tudor and Stuart
needlework.

24. *snail*] a traditional symbol of sexual power, often carried as a love
talisman.

32. *pop'ring pear tree*] The fruit of this tree, named for the town of
Poperinghe in Flanders, because of its shape was used often to signify male
sex organs. Cf. Shakespeare, *Romeo and Juliet*, II. i. 37–8:

  O Romeo! that she were, O! that she were
  An open '*et caetera*', thou a poperin pear.

creature she maintains, still seeming to play and dally
under the pop'ring so long that it has almost washed away
the earth from the root, and now the poor tree stands as if 40
it were ready to fall and perish by that whereon it spent all
the substance it had.

Cata. Moral for you that love those wanton running waters.

Seb. But is not my Lady Levidulcia come yet?

Cata. Her purpose promised us her company ere this. *Lirie,* 45
your lute and your book.

Seb. Well said. A lesson o' th' lute to entertain the time with
till she comes.

Cata. Sol, fa, mi, la—Mi, mi, mi—Precious! Dost not see *mi*
between the two crotchets? Strike me full there. So— 50
forward.—This is a sweet strain, and thou finger'st it
beastly. *Mi* is a large there, and the prick that stands
before *mi* a long; always halve your note. Now—run your
division pleasingly with those quavers. Observe all your
graces i' the touch. Here's a sweet close—strike it full; it 55
sets off your music delicately.

---

45. *Lirie*] *Q, Nicoll;* Sirrie *Collins;* Sirrah *Symonds.*   52. large] *Nicoll;*
laerg *Q.*   53. halve] *This ed.;* halfe *Q.*

41–2. *spent . . . substance*] (*a*) expended wealth, (*b*) emitted semen.

45. Lirie] Unexplained. There may be here, as Nicoll notes, some corruption in the text. Since Collins's emendation is not a very reasonable one,
I have allowed the quarto reading to stand.

52. *large*] a maxim, one kind of single note in the system of 'mensural
notation' developed by Franco of Cologne around 1250 and in use until
about 1600. Cf. R. C. Bald, in *M.L.R.*, XVI (1921), 324. The word is sug-
gestive also of sexual openness.

prick] (*a*) a dot placed after a note or rest in musical notation, (*b*) male
sex organ.

53. mi] (*a*) the musical note, (*b*) me.

54. *division*] (*a*) in music, the execution of a rapid melodic passage, conceived as the division of a series of long notes into shorter ones, (*b*) the
separation of the legs. The term was often used metaphorically. Cf. Marlowe, *The Jew of Malta* (ed. Brooke), 1846:

That kisse again; she runs division of my lips.

quavers] (*a*) in music, notes equal in length to half a crotchet or one-
eighth of a semibreve, (*b*) sexual thrills.

55. *graces*] (*a*) musical embellishments, (*b*) sexual dexterity.

close] (*a*) musical finale, (*b*) coition.

Enter LANGUEBEAU SNUFFE *and* LEVIDULCIA.

Lang. Purity be in this house.

Cata. 'Tis now entered, and welcome with your good ladyship.

Seb. Cease that music. Here's a sweeter instrument. [*Goes to* 60
embrace her.]

Lev. Restrain your liberty. See you not Snuffe?

Seb. What does the stinkard here? Put Snuffe out. He's
offensive.

Lev. No. The credit of his company defends my being abroad
from the eye of suspicion. 65

Cata. Will 't please your ladyship go up into the closet?
There are those falls and tires I told you of.

Lev. Monsieur Snuffe, I shall request your patience. My stay
will not be long. *Exit with* SEBASTIAN.

Lang. My duty, madam. Falls and tires? I begin to suspect 70
what falls and tires you mean. My lady and Sebastian the
fall and the tire, and I the shadow. I perceive the purity of
my conversation is used but for a property to cover the
uncleanness of their purposes. The very contemplation o'
the thing makes the spirit of the flesh begin to wriggle in 75
my blood. And here my desire has met with an object
already. This gentlewoman, methinks, should be swayed

69. *with* SEBASTIAN] *Symonds; cum Sebast. Q.*

---

62. *stinkard*] one who stinks, a common abusive term.

Snuffe] (*a*) an extinguished wick or candle end which must be removed,
(*b*) the odour created by such a candle end.

64. *credit*] good reputation.

67. *falls and tires*] ladies' headgear often the subject of Elizabethan word
play with sexual overtones. The fall was a veil worn in front of a bonnet,
the tire or tyre a special kind of hat. Cf. Marston, *The Malcontent* (ed.
Bullen), v. iii. 16–19:

Look ye, these tiring things are justly out of request now: and, do ye
hear? You must wear falling bands, you must come into the falling
fashion.

72. *shadow*] a bonegrace or border attached to a bonnet to protect a lady's
complexion.

73. *property*] instrument or means to an end.

75. *spirit of the flesh*] male sex organ.

with the motion, living in a house where moving example
is so common. Temptation has prevailed over me, and I
will attempt to make it overcome her.—Mistress Cata-   80
plasma, my lady, it seems, has some business that requires
her stay. The fairness o' the evening invites me into the
air; will it please you give this gentlewoman leave to leave
her work and walk a turn or two with me for honest
recreation?   85

Cata. With all my heart, sir. Go, Soquette, give ear to his
instructions. You may get understanding by his company, I can tell you.

Lang. In the way of holiness, Mistress Cataplasma.

Cata. Good Monsieur Snuffe! I will attend your return.   90

Lang. [*To* SOQUETTE] Your hand, gentlewoman.
　　　[*Aside*] The flesh is humble till the spirit move it,
　　　But when 'tis rais'd it will command above it.   *Exeunt.*

[IV. ii]

　　　　　Enter D'AMVILLE, CHARLEMONT, *and* BORACHIO.

D'Am. Your sadness and the sickness of my son
　　　Have made our company and conference
　　　Less free and pleasing than I purpos'd it.

Char. Sir, for the present I am much unfit
　　　For conversation or society.   5
　　　With pardon I will rudely take my leave.

D'Am. Good night, dear nephew.   *Exit* CHARLEMONT.
　　　　　　　　　　Seest thou that same man?

Bor. Your meaning, sir?

D'Am.　　　　　That fellow's life, Borachio,

79–80. Temptation . . . her] *Q; not in Collins, Symonds.*　91. *To* SOQUETTE]
Symonds.

---

78. *motion*] (*a*) suggestion, (*b*) emotion (*O.E.D.*). Cf. Shakespeare,
Othello, I. iii. 335–6:
　. . . but we have reason to cool our raging motions, our carnal stings, our
unbitted lusts.

    Like a superfluous letter in the law,

    Endangers our assurance.

Bor.   Scrape him out.   10

D'Am. Wou't do 't?

Bor.   Give me your purpose; I will do 't.

D'Am. Sad melancholy has drawn Charlemont,

    With meditation on his father's death,

    Into the solitary walk behind the church.

Bor. The churchyard? This the fittest place for death.   15

    Perhaps he's praying. Then he's fit to die.

    We'll send him charitably to his grave.

D'Am. No matter how thou tak'st him. First take this.

                              [Gives him a] pistol.

    Thou know'st the place. Observe his passages,

    And with the most advantage make a stand,   20

    That favour'd by the darkness of the night,

    His breast may fall upon thee at so near

    A distance that he sha' not shun the blow.

    The deed once done, thou may'st retire with safety.

    The place is unfrequented, and his death   25

    Will be imputed to th' attempt of thieves.

Bor. Be careless. Let your mind be free and clear.

    This pistol shall discharge you of your fear.   *Exit.*

D'Am. But let me call my projects to account,

    For what effect and end I have engag'd   30

---

11. Wou't] *This ed.;* Wut *Q, Nicoll;* Wilt *Collins.*   18.1. *Gives him a*]
Symonds.

---

9. *superfluous . . . law*] A single extra letter inserted in a law might modi-
fy the sense radically and so bring a man into danger.

11. *Wou't*] wilt.

16. *Perhaps . . . die*] As Collins suggests, this may be a reminiscence of
Shakespeare's *Hamlet*, III. iii. 73–84.

19. *passages*] the line of his walk.

20. *make a stand*] take up a position.

27. *careless*] free from care.

30–3. *For . . . continued*] M. C. Bradbrook, *Themes and Conventions of
Elizabethan Tragedy*, p. 177, points out the similarity of these lines to
Macbeth's concern over his posterity. Cf. Shakespeare, *Macbeth*, III. i.
61–70.

K

Myself in all this blood. To leave a state
To the succession of my proper blood.
But how shall that succession be continu'd?
Not in my elder son, I fear. Disease
And weakness have disabled him for issue.   35
For th' t'other, his loose humour will endure
No bond of marriage. And I doubt his life;
His spirit is so boldly dangerous.
O pity that the profitable end
Of such a prosp'rous murder should be lost!   40
Nature forbid. I hope I have a body
That will not suffer me to lose my labour
For want of issue yet. But then 't must be
A bastard. Tush, they only father bastards
That father other men's begettings. Daughter!   45
Be it mine own, let it come whence it will.
I am resolv'd. Daughter!

Enter Servant.

Ser.   My lord.
D'Am. I prithee call my daughter.

Enter CASTABELLA.

Cast. Your pleasure, sir?
D'Am.   Is thy husband i' bed?
Cast. Yes, my lord.
D'Am.   The evening's fair. I prithee   50
    Walk a turn or two.
Cast.   Come, Jaspar.
D'Am.   No.
    We'll walk but to the corner o' the church,

31. blood.] *Collins;* blood? *Q.*

---

31. *state*] estate.
32. *proper*] own.
37. *doubt*] fear for.
46. *Be it*] so long as it be.

And I have something to speak privately.

Cast. No matter; stay.   *Exit* Servant.

D'Am.   This falls out happily.   *Exeunt.*

[IV. iii]

Enter CHARLEMONT, BORACHIO *dogging him in the churchyard.*
The clock strikes twelve.

Char. Twelve.

Bor. 'Tis a good hour; 'twill strike one anon.

Char. How fit a place for contemplation is this dead of night,
among the dwellings of the dead.—This grave—perhaps
th' inhabitant was in his lifetime the possessor of his own   5
desires. Yet in the midst of all his greatness and his wealth
he was less rich and less contented than in this poor piece
of earth, lower and lesser than a cottage, for here he
neither wants nor cares.

Now that his body savours of corruption,   10
He enjoys a sweeter rest than e'er he did
Amongst the sweetest pleasures of this life,
For here there's nothing troubles him.—And there—
In that grave lies another. He, perhaps,
Was in his life as full of misery   15
As this of happiness, and here's an end
Of both. Now both their states are equal. O
That man with so much labour should aspire
To worldly height, when in the humble earth
The world's condition's at the best! Or scorn   20
Inferior men, since to be lower than
A worm is to be higher than a king.

IV. iii. 2. *strike one*] (*a*) strike one o'clock, (*b*) strike Charlemont.

3–22. *How . . . king*] This speech, although full of commonplaces of *contemptus mundi* moralizing, seems to be based in particular upon the graveyard scene (V. i.) in *Hamlet*.

10. *savours*] smells.

17. *states*] (*a*) conditions, (*b*) estates.

Bor. Then fall and rise.

                        Discharges [the pistol, which] gives false fire.

Char.   What villain's hand was that?

     Save thee or thou shalt perish.   *They fight.*

Bor.   Zounds, unsav'd, I think.

                                        Fall[s].

Char. What, have I kill'd him? Whatsoe'er thou beest,   25
     I would thy hand had prosper'd, for I was
     Unfit to live and well prepar'd to die.
     What shall I do? Accuse myself, submit
     Me to the law, and that will quickly end
     This violent increase of misery.   30
     But 'tis a murder to be accessory
     To mine own death. I will not. I will take
     This opportunity to 'scape. It may
     Be Heav'n reserves me to some better end.   *Exit.*

        Enter [LANGUEBEAU] SNUFFE *and* SOQUETTE
               into the churchyard.

Soq. Nay, good sir, I dare not. In good sooth I come of a   35
    generation both by father and mother that were all as
    fruitful as costermongers' wives.

Lang. Tush, then a tympany is the greatest danger can be
    feared. Their fruitfulness turns but to a certain kind of
    phlegmatic windy disease.   40

23.1. *the pistol, which*] *Symonds.*   37. costermongers'] *Symonds;* costard-mongers *Q.*

---

   23. *rise*] i.e., to heaven.
   23.1. gives false fire] misfires.
   24. *Save thee*] escape.   *unsav'd*] (*a*) not escaped, (*b*) damned.
   38. *tympany*] a swelling or tumour of any sort. The *double entendre* is a common one. Cf. Nashe, *A Prognostication* (ed. McKerrow, rev. Wilson), III, 384–5:
    . . . some shalbe so short heeld & so quesie stomackt that they shal ly in their beds while noon, by the which means they shal grow so ful of grosse humors that they shalbe troubled with strange timpanies & swelling in their bellies, vncurable for forty weekes vntill they be helped by the aduice of some skilfull Midwife.
   40. *phlegmatic*] composed of phlegm, and therefore, according to the old

Soq. I must put my understanding to your trust, sir. I would
    be loath to be deceived.

Lang. No, conceive thou sha't not. Yet thou shalt profit by my
    instruction too. My body is not every day drawn dry,
    wench.   45

Soq. Yet methinks, sir, your want of use should rather make
    your body like a well: the lesser 'tis drawn, the sooner it
    grows dry.

Lang. Thou shalt try that instantly.

Soq. But we want place and opportunity.   50

Lang. We have both. This is the back side of the house which
    the superstitious call Saint Winifred's church, and is
    verily a convenient unfrequented place,
    Where under the close curtains of the night—

Soq. You purpose i' the dark to make me light.   55
        [SNUFFE] *pulls out a sheet, a hair, and a beard.*
    But what ha' you there?

Lang. This disguise is for security sake, wench. There's a
    talk, thou know'st, that the ghost of old Montferrers
    walks. In this church he was buried. Now if any stranger
    fall upon us before our business be ended, in this disguise   60
    I shall be taken for that ghost and never be called to
    examination, I warrant thee. Thus we shall 'scape both
    prevention and discovery. How do I look in this habit,
    wench?

Soq. So like a ghost that, notwithstanding I have some fore-   65
    knowledge of you, you make my hair stand almost on end.

---

43. conceive] *Collins;* conceive; *Q.*   55.1. SNUFFE] *Symonds.*   66. on]
Collins; an *Q.*

---

physiology, lethargic and dull. The sense of the passage is that the fruitful-
ness of the parents in the next generation produces only a swelling composed of air and phlegm (largely water).

    41. *understanding*] (*a*) comprehension, (*b*) lying under.

    43. *conceive*] (*a*) understand, (*b*) conceive a child.

    47–8. *drawn . . . dry*] Cf. Tilley, W262: 'Drawn wells are seldom dry'.

    55. *light*] i.e., a whore.

    55.1. *hair*] wig.

Lang. I will try how I can kiss in this beard.—O, fie, fie, fie.
I will put it off, and then kiss, and then put it on. I can do
the rest without kissing.

Enter CHARLEMONT *doubtfully, with his sword drawn. [He] is upon
them before they are aware. They run out divers ways and leave the
disguise.*

Char. What ha' we here ? A sheet, a hair, a beard ?   70
What end was this disguise intended for ?
No matter what. I'll not expostulate
The purpose of a friendly accident.
Perhaps it may accommodate my 'scape.
I fear I am pursu'd. For more assurance,   75
I'll hide me here i' th' charnel house,
This convocation-house of dead men's skulls.

> *To get into the charnel house he takes hold
> of a death's head; it slips and staggers him.*

Death's head, deceiv'st my hold ?
Such is the trust to all mortality.

> *Hides himself in the charnel house.*

Enter D'AMVILLE *and* CASTABELLA.

Cast. My lord, the night grows late. Your lordship spake   80
Of something you desir'd to move in private.
D'Am. Yes, now I'll speak it. Th' argument is love.
The smallest ornament of thy sweet form,
That abstract of all pleasure, can command
The senses into passion, and thy entire   85
Perfection is my object; yet I love
Thee with the freedom of my reason. I
Can give thee reason for my love.
Cast.   Love me,

69.1. *drawn. He*] *This ed.; drawne, Q.*

69.1. *doubtfully*] fearfully.
72. *expostulate*] demand or question.
81. *move*] propose.

My lord ? I do believe it, for I am
The wife of him you love.

D'Am.   'Tis true. By my   90
Persuasion thou wert forc'd to marry one
Unable to perform the office of
A husband. I was author of the wrong.
My conscience suffers under 't, and I would
Disburden it by satisfaction.

Cast.   How ?   95

D'Am. I will supply that pleasure to thee which
He cannot.

Cast.   Are y' a devil or a man ?

D'Am. A man, and such a man as can return
Thy entertainment with as prodigal
A body as the covetous desire   100
Of woman ever was delighted with ;
So that, besides the full performance of
Thy empty husband's duty, thou shalt have
The joy of children to continue the
Succession of thy blood ; for the appetite   105
That steals her pleasure, draws the forces of
The body to an united strength and puts
'Em altogether into action,
Never fails of procreation.
All the purposes of man   110
Aim but at one of these two ends, pleasure

---

95. *it*] i.e., his conscience.
satisfaction] proper repayment.
99. *prodigal*] lavish in its giving of itself.
103. *empty*] (*a*) impotent, (*b*) foolish (*O.E.D.*).
105–9. *for . . . procreation*] Cf. Shakespeare, *King Lear*, I. ii. 9–15:
              Why brand they us
        With base ? with baseness ? bastardy ? base, base ?
        Who in the lusty stealth of nature take
        More composition and fierce quality
        Than doth, within a dull, stale, tired bed,
        Go to the creating a whole tribe of fops,
        Got 'tween asleep and wake ?

Or profit, and in this one sweet conjunction
Of our loves they both will meet. Would it
Not grieve thee that a stranger to thy blood
Should lay the first foundation of his house   115
Upon the ruins of thy family?

Cast. Now Heav'n defend me! May my memory
Be utterly extinguish'd, and the heir
Of him that was my father's enemy
Raise his eternal monument upon   120
Our ruins, ere the greatest pleasure or
The greatest profit ever tempt me to
Continue it by incest.

D'Am.   Incest, tush!
These distances affinity observes
Are articles of bondage cast upon   125
Our freedoms by our own subjections.
Nature allows a gen'ral liberty
Of generation to all creatures else.
Shall man, to whose command and use all creatures
Were made subject, be less free than they?   130

Cast. O God,
Is thy unlimited and infinite
Omnipotence less free because thou dost
No ill? Or if you argue merely out
Of Nature, do you not degenerate   135
From that, and are you not unworthy the
Prerogative of Nature's masterpiece,
When basely you prescribe yourself
Authority and law from their examples

incest as
freedom

123–30. *Incest . . . they*] The source of this argument, as Collins indicates,
is Book x of Ovid's *Metamorphoses*. Cf. Arthur Golding's translation (1567)
[Sig. R8ʳ]:

For euery other liuing wyght dame nature doth permit
To match without offence of sin. The heefer thinkes no shame
To beare her father on her back: The horse bestrydes the same
Of whom he is the syre *etc.*

124. *affinity*] kinship.
126. *subjections*] submissions.

Whom you should command? I could confute   140
You, but the horror of the argument
Confounds my understanding.—Sir, I know
You do but try me in your son's behalf,
Suspecting that my strength and youth of blood
Cannot contain themselves with impotence.   145
Believe me, sir,
I never wrong'd him. If it be your lust,
O quench it on their prostituted flesh,
Whose trade of sin can please desire with more
Delight and less offence.—The poison of   150
Your breath, evaporated from so foul a soul,
Infects the air more than the damps that rise
From bodies but half rotten in their graves.

D'Am. Kiss me. I warrant thee my breath is sweet.
These dead men's bones lie here of purpose to   155
Invite us to supply the number of
The living. Come, we'll get young bones and do 't.
I will enjoy thee. No? Nay then invoke
Your great suppos'd protector. I will do 't.

Cast. Suppos'd protector? Are y' an atheist? Then   160
I know my prayers and tears are spent in vain.
O patient Heav'n, why dost thou not express
Thy wrath in thunderbolts, to tear the frame
Of man in pieces? How can earth endure
The burden of this wickedness without   165
An earthquake, or the angry face of Heav'n
Be not enflam'd with lightning?

D'Am.   Conjure up
The devil and his dam; cry to the graves;
The dead can hear thee; invocate their help.

Cast. O would this grave might open, and my body   170
Were bound to the dead carcass of a man
For ever, ere it entertain the lust

---

152. *damps*] noxious vapours or gases.
157. *get*] beget.

Of this detested villain.

D'Am.   Tereus-like,
Thus I will force my passage to—

Char.   The devil!

CHARLEMONT *rises in the disguise and frights* D'AMVILLE *away.*

Now lady, with the hand of Charlemont   175
I thus redeem you from the arm of lust.
My Castabella!

Cast.   My dear Charlemont!

Char. For all my wrongs I thank thee, gracious Heav'n;
Th' hast made me satisfaction, to reserve
Me for this blessed purpose. Now, sweet death,   180
I'll bid thee welcome. Come, I'll guard thee home,
And then I'll cast myself into the arms
Of apprehension, that the law may make
This worthy work the crown of all my actions,
Being the best and last.

Cast.   The last? The law?   185
Now Heav'n forbid, what ha' you done?

Char.   Why, I have kill'd
A man, not murder'd him, my Castabella;
He would ha' murder'd me.

Cast.   Then, Charlemont,
The hand of Heav'n directed thy defence.
That wicked atheist, I suspect his plot.   190

Char. My life he seeks. I would he had it, since
He has depriv'd me of those blessings that
Should make me love it. Come, I'll give it him.

Cast. You sha' not. I will first expose myself
To certain danger than for my defence   195
Destroy the man that sav'd me from destruction.

173. Tereus] Tereas *Q.*

---

173. *Tereus*] the ravisher of Philomela in the Greek myth.
179. *satisfaction*] Cf. IV. iii. 95.
reserve] keep especially.
183. *apprehension*] arrest by officers of the law.

Char. Thou canst not satisfy me better than
         To be the instrument of my release
         From misery.
Cast.   Then work it by escape.
         Leave me to this protection that still guards   200
         The innocent, or I will be a partner
         In your destiny.
Char. My soul is heavy. Come, lie down to rest;
         These are the pillows whereon men sleep best.

> *They lie down with either of them*
> *a death's head for a pillow.*

Enter [LANGUEBEAU] SNUFFE *seeking* SOQUETTE.

Lang. Soquette, Soquette, Soquette! O art thou there?   205

> *He mistakes the body of* BORACHIO *for* SOQUETTE.

Verily thou liest in a fine premeditate readiness for the
purpose. Come, kiss me, sweet Soquette.—Now purity
defend me from the sin of Sodom! This is a creature of
the masculine gender.—Verily the man is blasted.—Yea,
cold and stiff!—Murder, murder, murder.   *Exit.* 210

> *Enter* D'AMVILLE *distractedly;* [*he*] *starts at the sight*
> *of a death's head.*

D'Am. Why dost thou stare upon me? Thou art not
         The skull of him I murder'd. What hast thou
         To do to vex my conscience? Sure thou wert
         The head of a most dogged usurer,
         Th' art so uncharitable. And that bawd,   215
         The sky there, she could shut the windows and

210.1. *he*] Symonds.

---

200. *still*] always.
206. *premeditate*] deliberate.
211. *Why . . . me*] Cf. Shakespeare, *Macbeth*, III. iv. 50–1:
          Thou canst not say I did it: never shake
          Thy gory locks at me.
214. *dogged*] dog-like.

The doors of this great chamber of the world,
And draw the curtains of the clouds between
Those lights and me about this bed of earth,
When that same strumpet, Murder, and myself   220
Committed sin together. Then she could
Leave us i' the dark till the close deed
Was done, but now that I begin to feel
The loathsome horror of my sin and, like
A lecher empty'd of his lust, desire   225
To bury my face under my eyebrows and
Would steal from my shame unseen, she meets me
I' the face with all her light corrupted eyes
To challenge payment o' me. O behold!
Yonder's the ghost of old Montferrers in   230
A long white sheet, climbing yond' lofty mountain
To complain to Heav'n of me. Montferrers!
'Pox o' fearfulness. 'Tis nothing but
A fair white cloud. Why, was I born a coward?
He lies that says so. Yet the count'nance of   235
A bloodless worm might ha' the courage now
To turn my blood to water. The trembling motion
Of an aspen leaf would make me, like
The shadow of that leaf, lie shaking under 't.
I could now commit a murder, were   240
It but to drink the fresh warm blood of him
I murder'd, to supply the want and weakness
O' mine own, 'tis grown so cold and phlegmatic.
Lang. Murder, murder, murder.   *Within.*
D'Am. Mountains o'erwhelm me; the ghost of old Mont- 245
ferrers haunts me.

---

222. *close*] secret, hidden.
223–4. *feel . . . sin*] Cf. Shakespeare, *Macbeth*, v. ii. 16–17:
                    Now does he feel
          His secret murders sticking on his hands.
229. *challenge*] demand.
245. *Mountains o'erwhelm me*] Cf. Marlowe, *Doctor Faustus* (ed. Jump),
xix. 152:

Lang. Murder, murder, murder.

D'Am. O were my body circumvolv'd
Within that cloud, that when the thunder tears
His passage open, it might scatter me   250
To nothing in the air!

            Enter LANGUEBEAU SNUFFE *with the* Watch.

Lang.   Here you shall find
The murder'd body.

D'Am.   Black Beelzebub
And all his hell-hounds come to apprehend me?

Lang. No, my good lord, we come to apprehend
The murderer.

D'Am.   The ghost, great Pluto, was   255
A fool, unfit to be employ'd in any
Serious business for the state of hell.
Why could not he ha' suffer'd me to raise
The mountain o' my sins with one as damnable

_____

255. *D'Am.*] *Collins; not in* Q.   258. Why] *Collins;* Why? Q.

_____

Mountains and hills, come, come, and fall on me.
Jump calls attention to Revelation vi. 16: 'And said to the mountains and
the rocks, Fall on us, and hide us from the face of him that sitteth on the
throne, and from the wrath of the Lamb'. There may be also in Tourneur's
image a suggestion of the classical legend of Jove's destruction of the giants
who warred against him, foreshadowing D'Amville's similar destruction as
the foe of God.

248-51. O . . . air] M. C. Bradbrook, *Themes and Conventions of Elizabethan Tragedy*, p. 177, has compared this speech to the dying Faustus'
plea for bodily dissolution. Cf. Marlowe, *Doctor Faustus* (ed. Jump), xix.
157-63:

            You stars that reign'd at my nativity,
            Whose influence hath allotted death and hell,
            Now draw up Faustus like a foggy mist
            Into the entrails of yon labouring cloud,
            That, when you vomit forth into the air,
            My limbs may issue from your smoky mouths,
            So that my soul may but ascend to heaven.

It is interesting that Marlowe had used the same categories of imagery
upon which Tourneur relies so heavily throughout his play: stars, clouds,
thunder. Cf. Introduction, pp. xliii-xlvi.

248. *circumvolv'd*] enveloped.

As all the rest, and then ha' tumbled me   260
To ruin? But apprehend me e'en between
The purpose and the act, before it was
Committed!

Watch. Is this the murderer? He speaks suspiciously.

Lang. No, verily. This is my Lord D'Amville, and his dis-   265
traction, I think, grows out of his grief for the loss of a
faithful servant, for surely I take him to be Borachio that
is slain.

D'Am. Ha! Borachio slain? Thou look'st like Snuffe, dost
not?   270

Lang. Yes, in sincerity, my lord.

D'Am. Hark thee—sawest thou not a ghost?

Lang. A ghost? Where, my lord? [*Aside*] I smell a fox.

D'Am. Here i' the churchyard.

Lang. Tush, tush, their walking spirits are mere imaginary   275
fables. There's no such thing in *rerum natura*. Here is a
man slain, and with the spirit of consideration I rather
think him to be the murderer got into that disguise than
any such fantastic toy.

D'Am. My brains begin to put themselves in order. I appre-   280
hend thee now. 'Tis e'en so.—Borachio!—I will search
the centre, but I'll find the murderer.

Watch. Here, here, here.

D'Am. Stay. Asleep? So soundly? And so sweetly upon
death's heads? And in a place so full of fear and horror?   285
Sure there is some other happiness within the freedom

---

273. *smell a fox*] am suspicious.

276. rerum natura] a probable allusion to Lucretius, *De Rerum Natura*,
regarded by Tourneur's contemporaries as a virtual handbook of atheism.

279. *toy*] foolish product of the imagination. Cf. Shakespeare, *Hamlet*,
I. iv. 75–8:

> The very place puts toys of desperation,
> Without more motive, into every brain
> That looks so many fathoms to the sea
> And hears it roar beneath.

282. *centre*] of the earth.

of the conscience than my knowledge e'er attained to.—
Ho, ho, ho!

Char. Y' are welcome, uncle. Had you sooner come,
You had been sooner welcome. I'm the man   290
You seek. You sha' not need examine me.

D'Am. My nephew! And my daughter! O my dear
Lamented blood, what fate has cast you thus
Unhappily upon this accident?

Char. You know, sir, she's as clear as chastity.   295

D'Am. As her own chastity. The time, the place,
All circumstances argue that unclear.

Cast. Sir, I confess it, and repentantly
Will undergo the selfsame punishment
That justice shall inflict on Charlemont.   300

Char. Unjustly she betrays her innocence.

Watch. But, sir, she's taken with you, and she must
To prison with you.

D'Am.   There's no remedy,
Yet were it not my son's bed she abus'd,
My land should fly but both should be excus'd. *Exeunt.*   305

[IV. iv]

Enter BELFOREST *and a* Servant.

Bel. Is not my wife come in yet?
Ser.   No, my lord.
Bel. Methinks she's very affectedly inclin'd
To young Sebastian's company o' late,
But jealousy is such a torment that
I am afraid to entertain it. Yet   5
The more I shun by circumstance to meet

---

305. *fly*] no longer be mine. Cf. Marlowe, *Edward II* (ed. Brooke), 998:
    Wigmore shall flie, to set my vnckle free.

IV. iv. 6–8. *The more . . . apprehension*] i.e., the more I strive to avoid
occasion for jealousy, the more reason for such striving is given to me (as
the causes for suspicion increase).
    6. *by circumstance*] by going roundabout.

Directly with it, the more ground I find
To circumvent my apprehension. First
I know sh' has a perpetual appetite,
Which being so oft encounter'd with a man   10
Of such a bold luxurious freedom as
Sebastian is, and of so promising
A body, her own blood, corrupted, will
Betray her to temptation.

Enter FRESCO *closely.*

Fres. [*Aside*] 'Precious! I was sent by his lady to see if her   15
lord were in bed. I should ha' done 't slyly without discovery, and now I am blurted upon 'em before I was
aware.   *Exit.*

Bel. Know not you the gentlewoman my wife brought home ?

Ser. By sight, my lord. Her man was here but now.   20

Bel. Her man ? I prithee run and call him quickly. [*Exit* Servant.]
This villain, I suspect him ever since I found him hid
behind the tapestry.

[*Enter* FRESCO *with* Servant.]

Fresco! Th' art welcome, Fresco. Leave us.   [*Exit* Servant.]
Dost hear, Fresco ? Is not my wife at thy mistress's ?   25

Fres. I know not, my lord.

Bel. I prithee tell me, Fresco, we are private, tell me. Is not thy
mistress a good wench ?

Fres. How means your lordship that ? A wench o' the trade ?

Bel. Yes faith, Fresco, e'en a wench o' the trade.   30

Fres. O no, my lord. Those falling diseases cause baldness,

14.1. FRESCO] Frisco *Q* (*and throughout scene*).   21. prithee] pr'ithee *Q*.
23.1. *Enter . . . Servant*] *This ed.; Re-enter* FRESCO *Symonds.*   24. *Exit*
Servant] *Symonds.*

---

11. *luxurious*] lecherous.
14.1. closely] quietly, trying to avoid notice.
16–17. *discovery*] being discovered.
31. *falling diseases*] (*a*) epilepsy, (*b*) diseases caused by lying down, i.e.,
syphilis, believed to cause baldness. For a good view of contemporary
notions about this disease, see *The Hunting of the Pox* (1619) by J. T.

and my mistress recovers the loss of hair, for she is a peri-
wig maker.

Bel. And nothing else?

Fres. Sells falls and tires and bodies for ladies, or so.   35

Bel. So, sir, and she helps my lady to falls and bodies now and
then, does she not?

Fres. At her ladyship's pleasure, my lord.

Bel. Her pleasure, you rogue? You are the pander to her pleasure, you varlet, are you not? You know the conveyances   40
between Sebastian and my wife. Tell me the truth, or by
this hand I'll nail thy bosom to the earth. Stir not, you
dog, but quickly tell the truth.

Fres. O yes!   *Speak[s] like a crier.*

Bel. Is not thy mistress a bawd to my wife?   45

Fres. O yes!

Bel. And acquainted with her tricks and her plots and her
devices?

Fres. O yes! If any man, court, city or country, has found my
Lady Levidulcia in bed but my Lord Belforest, it is   50
Sebastian.

Bel. What, dost thou proclaim it? Dost thou cry it, thou
villain?

Fres. Can you laugh it, my lord? I thought you meant to proclaim yourself cuckold.   55

Enter the Watch.

Bel. The watch! Met with my wish. I must request th' assistance of your offices.   FRESCO *runs away.*
'Sdeath, stay that villain; pursue him.   *Exeunt.*

---

49. court] *This ed.;* 'court *Q, Nicoll;* o'court *Collins.*

---

35. *falls and tires*] Cf. IV. i. 67.
bodies] bodices (with a glance at the selling of bodies in prostitution).
40. *conveyances*] (*a*) carrying of messages, (*b*) carrying on of affairs.
44. *O yes*] Fresco mimics the 'Oyez' of the town crier.
54. *laugh it*] say it laughingly, antithetic to 'cry it' (52), which suggests
(*a*) proclaim it, (*b*) weep it.

L

[IV. v]

Enter [LANGUEBEAU] SNUFFE *importuning* SOQUETTE.

Soq. Nay, if you get me any more into the churchyard—

Lang. Why, Soquette, I never got thee there yet.

Soq. Got me there? No, not with child.

Lang. I promised thee I would not, and I was as good as my
     word.   5

Soq. Yet your word was better then than your deed. But steal
     up into the little matted chamber o' the left hand.

Lang. I prithee let it be the right hand; thou left'st me before,
     and I did not like that.

Soq. 'Precious, quickly—so soon as my mistress shall be in   10
     bed I'll come to you.   *Exit* [LANGUEBEAU] SNUFFE.

Enter SEBASTIAN, LEVIDULCIA *and* CATAPLASMA.

Cata. I wonder Fresco stays so long.

Seb.   Mistress
     Soquette, a word with you.   *Whisper*[*s*].

Lev.   If he brings word
     My husband is i' bed, I will adventure
     One night's liberty to lie abroad.—   15
     My strange affection to this man! 'Tis like

IV. v. 1. churchyard—] *This ed.;* Churchyard. *Q, Nicoll;* Churchyard!
Collins.   2. *Lang.*] *Snu. Q (and throughout scene).*

   IV. v. 7. *matted*] Cf. I. iv. 146.
   14. *adventure*] i.e., take.
   16–22. *'Tis . . . for 't*] Levidulcia sees love in purely animal terms as a
physical compulsion beyond human control. Tourneur may here be re-
acting against Chapman's description of Tamyra's love for Bussy. Cf.
Bussy D'Ambois (ed. Parrott), II. ii. 140–1:
             You know, besides, that our affection's storm,
             Rais'd in our blood, no reason can reform.
III. i. 62–6:
             It is not I, but urgent destiny,
             That (as great statesmen for their general end
             In politic justice, make poor men offend)
             Enforceth my offence to make it just.
             What shall weak dames do, when the whole work of nature
             Hath a strong finger in each of us?

That natural sympathy which e'en among
The senseless creatures of the earth commands
A mutual inclination and consent.
For though it seems to be the free effect   20
Of mine own voluntary love, yet I
Can neither restrain it, nor give reason for 't.
But now 'tis done, and in your power it lies
To save my honour or dishonour me.

Cata. Enjoy your pleasure, madam, without fear.   25
I never will betray the trust you have
Committed to me, and you wrong yourself
To let consideration of the sin
Molest your conscience. Methinks 'tis unjust
That a reproach should be inflicted on   30
A woman for offending but with one,
When 'tis a light offence in husbands to
Commit with many.

Lev.   So it seems to me.—
Why, how now, Sebastian, making love to that gentlewoman ? How many mistresses ha' you i' faith ?   35

Seb. In faith, none, for I think none of 'em are faithful, but
otherwise, as many as clean shirts. The love of a woman is
like a mushroom; it grows in one night and will serve
somewhat pleasingly next morning to breakfast, but
afterwards waxes fulsome and unwholesome.   40

Cata. Nay, by Saint Winifred, a woman's love lasts as long as
winter fruit.

Seb. 'Tis true—till new come in, by my experience no longer.

Enter FRESCO *running*.

39. next] *Q* (*uncorrected*); 'next *Q* (*corrected*).   43. true—] *Collins;* true.
Q.

---

42. *winter fruit*] either preserved fruit or very late grown fruit of poor
quality, not likely to last very long. The expression seems to have been a
common one. Cf. Webster, *The White Devil* (ed. Brown), v. vi. 64–5:
          I'll stop your throat
With winter plums.

Fres. Somebody's doing has undone us, and we are like pay
    dearly for 't.   45
Seb. Pay dear ? For what ?
Fres. Will 't not be a chargeable reckoning, think you, when
    here are half a dozen fellows coming to call us to account,
    with ev'ry man a several bill in his hand that we are not
    able to discharge.   *Knock at the door.* 50
Cata. Passion o' me, what bouncing's that ? Madam, with-
    draw yourself.
Lev. Sebastian, if you love me, save my honour.
                          Exeunt [all except SEBASTIAN].

Enter BELFOREST *and the* Watch.

Seb. What violence is this ? What seek you ? Zounds, you
    shall not pass.   55
Bel. Pursue the strumpet. [*Exeunt* Watch.] Villain, give me way,
    Or I will make my passage through thy blood.
Seb. My blood will make it slippery, my lord.
    'Twere better you would take another way.
    You may hap fall else.
          They fight. Both [are] slain. SEBASTIAN *falls first.*
          I ha 't i' faith.   *Dies.* 60

While BELFOREST *is staggering, enter* LEVIDULCIA.

Lev. O God! My husband! My Sebastian! Husband!
    Neither can speak; yet both report my shame.

44. like] *Q;* like to *Collins.*   48. account] *Symonds;* accompt *Q.*
53.1. *all except* SEBASTIAN] *Symonds.*   53.2. *Enter . . .* Watch] *This ed.;*
after l. 55 *Q.*   56. *Exeunt* Watch] *This ed.*   60.1. *are*] *Symonds.*   60. I
ha 't] *Seba.* I ha't *Q.*

---

    49. *bill*] (*a*) weapon made of a concave blade or axe-head fixed to a pole,
(*b*) written demand for payment.
    50. *discharge*] pay. (The commercial metaphor should be noted.)
    51. *bouncing*] noisy knocking. Cf. s.d. in Marlowe, *Doctor Faustus* (ed.
Jump), xvii, 35:
        The Clowns *bounce at the gate within.*
    60. *hap*] happen to.

Is this the saving of my honour, when
Their blood runs out in rivers, and my lust
The fountain whence it flows ? Dear husband, let   65
Not thy departed spirit be displeas'd
If with adult'rate lips I kiss thy cheek.
Here I behold the hatefulness of lust,
Which brings me kneeling to embrace him dead,
Whose body living I did loathe to touch.   70
Now I can weep. But what can tears do good ?
When I weep only water, they weep blood.
But could I make an ocean with my tears,
That on the flood this broken vessel of
My body, laden heavy with light lust,   75
Might suffer shipwreck and so drown my shame,
Then weeping were to purpose; but alas,
The sea wants water enough to wash away
The foulness of my name. O, in their wounds
I feel my honour wounded to the death.   80
Shall I outlive my honour ? Must my life
Be made the world's example ? Since it must,
Then thus in detestation of my deed,
To make th' example move more forcibly
To virtue, thus I seal it with a death   85

78-9. *The ... name*] Cf. Shakespeare, *Macbeth*, II. ii. 61-4:
> Will all great Neptune's ocean wash this blood
> Clean from my hand ? No, this my hand will rather
> The multitudinous seas incarnadine,
> Making the green one red.

Collins suggests that Levidulcia's death speech was based on the final speeches of Marston's Isabella in *The Insatiate Countess*, v. i. Cf. in particular:
> Murder and lust, down with my ashes sink
> But, like ingrateful seed, perish in earth,
> That you may never spring against my soul,
> Like weeds to choke it in the heavenly harvest.

The Insatiate Countess was not printed until 1613, although it may have been written somewhat earlier. Anthony Caputi, *John Marston, Satirist* (Ithaca, N.Y., 1961), pp. 272-5, argues that Marston's contribution to this play (completed by William Barksteed) was a very small one and all written between 1606 and 1608.

As full of horror as my life of sin.   *Stabs herself.*

Enter the Watch *with* CATAPLASMA, FRESCO, [LANGUEBEAU]
SNUFFE *and* SOQUETTE.

Watch. Hold, madam! Lord, what a strange night is this!
Lang. May not Snuffe be suffered to go out of himself?
Watch. Nor you, nor any. All must go with us.
  O with what virtue lust should be withstood,   90
  Since 'tis a fire quench'd seldom without blood.   *Exeunt.*

---

88. *Snuffe . . . out*] Cf. IV. i. 62.

Act V

[v. i]

Music. A closet discovered. A Servant *sleeping with lights and money before him. Enter* D'AMVILLE.

D'*Am.* What, sleep'st thou?
Ser.   No, my lord, nor sleep nor wake,
    But in a slumber troublesome to both.
D'*Am.* Whence comes this gold?
Ser.   'Tis part of the revenue
    Due to your lordship since your brother's death.
D'*Am.* To bed. Leave me my gold.
Ser.   And me my rest.   5
    Two things wherewith one man is seldom blest.   *Exit.*
D'*Am.* Cease that harsh music. W' are not pleas'd with it.
                          He handles the gold.
    Here sounds a music whose melodious touch
    Like angels' voices ravishes the sense.
    Behold, thou ignorant astronomer,   10
    Whose wand'ring speculation seeks among
    The planets for men's fortunes! With amazement
    Behold thine error and be planet-struck.
    These are the stars whose operations make

Act v] Actus quinti Scena prima *Q.*

8–26. *Here . . . subordinate*] D'Amville's handling of his gold should be compared with the similar scenes of Barabas and Volpone in their counting houses. Cf. Marlowe, *The Jew of Malta* (ed. Brooke), 1–82; Jonson, *Volpone* (ed. Herford and Simpson), I. i. 1–27.

13. *planet-struck*] amazed by the influence of the pieces of gold (here compared with planets in their effect on men). Cf. Tilley, P389; Jonson, *Every Man in his Humour* (1601) (ed. Herford and Simpson), IV. ii. 125–6:
    Sure I was strooke with a plannet then, for I had no power to touch
    my weapon.

The fortunes and the destinies of men.   15
Yond' lesser eyes of Heav'n, like subjects rais'd
Into their lofty houses when their prince
Rides underneath th' ambition of their loves,
Are mounted only to behold the face
Of your more rich imperious eminence   20
With unprevented sight. Unmask, fair queen;

Unpurses the gold.

Vouchsafe their expectations may enjoy
The gracious favour they admire to see.
These are the stars, the ministers of fate,
And man's high wisdom the superior power   25
To which their forces are subordinate.   .   *Sleeps.*

Enter the GHOST OF MONTFERRERS.

Mont. D'Amville, with all thy wisdom th' art a fool,
Not like those fools that we term innocents,
But a most wretched miserable fool,
Which instantly, to the confusion of   30
Thy projects, with despair thou shalt behold.   *Exit.*

D'AMVILLE *starts up.*

D'Am. What foolish dream dares interrupt my rest
To my confusion? How can that be, since
My purposes have hitherto been borne
With prosp'rous judgment to secure success—   35
Which nothing lives to dispossess me of
But apprehended Charlemont, and him
This brain has made the happy instrument
To free suspicion, to annihilate
All interest and title of his own,   40
To seal up my assurance and confirm

21.1. *Unpurses the gold*] *Q (corrected); not in Q (uncorrected).*

---

18. *Rides underneath*] rides in a procession with spectators watching from windows above.
21. *unprevented*] unhindered.
28. *fools . . . innocents*] Innocents was a term used both for children and for half-witted people not responsible for their own acts (*O.E.D.*).

My absolute possession by the law.
Thus while the simple, honest worshipper
Of a fantastic providence groans under
The burden of neglected misery,   45
My real wisdom has rais'd up a state
That shall eternize my posterity.

Enter Servants *with the body of* SEBASTIAN.

What's that?
Ser.   The body of your younger son,
Slain by the Lord Belforest.
D'Am.   Slain? You lie.
Sebastian! Speak, Sebastian! H' has lost   50
His hearing. A physician presently!
Go, call a surgeon.
Rous.   O.   *Within.*
D'Am.   What groan was that?
How does my elder son? The sound came from
His chamber.
Ser.   He went sick to bed, my lord.
Rous. O.   *Within.*
D'Am. The cries of mandrakes never touch'd the ear   56
With more sad horror than that voice does mine.

Enter a Servant *running.*

52. O] Ooh *Q.*

---

56. *cries of mandrakes*] Collins cites Thomas Newton, *An Herbal for the Bible* (1587) [Sig. B5ᵛ–C1ᵛ], where the characteristics of this plant and Elizabethan beliefs about it are presented in considerable detail. It was said to have sprung in damp grounds from the seed of executed felons, to shriek when pulled out of the ground, causing any who heard it to go mad, and to possess various medicinal powers. To avoid madness one must gather the plant at midnight in a prescribed manner with the help of a dog. Allusions to mandrake in seventeenth-century literature are extremely numerous, but cf., in particular, Webster, *Duchess of Malfi* (ed. Lucas), II. v. 1–3:
Ferd. I have this night dig'd up a man-drake.
Car. Say you?
Ferd. And I am growne mad with 't.

Ser. If ever you will see your son alive—
D'Am. Nature forbid I e'er should see him dead.

A bed drawn forth with ROUSARD.

Withdraw the curtains. O how does my son ?   60
Ser. Methinks he's ready to give up the ghost.
D'Am. Destruction take thee and thy fatal tongue.
   Death! Where's the doctor ? Art not thou the face
   Of that prodigious apparition star'd upon
   Me in my dream ?
Ser.   The doctor's come, my lord.   65

Enter Doctor.

D'Am. Doctor, behold two patients in whose cure
   Thy skill may purchase an eternal fame.
   If thou hast any reading in Hippocrates,
   Galen or Avicen, if herbs or drugs
   Or minerals have any power to save,   70
   Now let thy practice and their sovereign use
   Raise thee to wealth and honour.
Doct.   If any root
   Of life remains within 'em capable
   Of physic, fear 'em not, my lord.

---

58. If ever] *Q (corrected), Nicoll;* Never *Q (uncorrected), Collins.*

---

60. *curtains*] of the bed. As the s.d. indicates, a bed was literally drawn
forth upon the stage with Rousard in it, as was common in death scenes on
the Elizabethan stage. Cf. the s.d. in Marlowe, *Massacre at Paris* (ed.
Brooke), 256: *Enter the Admirall in his bed.*
68–9. *Hippocrates, Galen, Avicen*] authorities on medicine throughout
the Middle Ages. Hippocrates (460 ?–377 B.C.) was a Greek physician,
known as 'Father of Medicine', said to have devised a code of ethics which
he imposed upon his disciples; eighty-seven medical treatises are attributed
to him. Galen (2nd century A.D.) was a Greek physician who settled in
Rome in A.D. 164, and of whose many medical treatises about a hundred are
extant. Avicenna (Ali al-Husayn ibn-Sina) was an Arab physician and
philosopher who travelled widely and wrote about a hundred works, his
greatest medical treatise being *The Canon*; he wrote also on theology, metaphysics, logic, and mathematics.

Rous.   O.

D'Am. His gasping sighs are like the falling noise   75
  Of some great building when the groundwork breaks.
  On these two pillars stood the stately frame
  And architecture of my lofty house.
  An earthquake shakes 'em; the foundation shrinks.
  Dear Nature, in whose honour I have rais'd   80
  A work of glory to posterity,
  O bury not the pride of that great action
  Under the fall and ruin of itself.

Doct. My lord, these bodies are depriv'd of all
  The radical ability of nature.   85
  The heat of life is utterly extinguish'd.
  Nothing remains within the power of man
  That can restore them.

D'Am.   Take this gold; extract
  The spirit of it, and inspire new life
  Into their bodies.

Doct.   Nothing can, my lord.   90

D'Am. You ha' not yet examin'd the true state
  And constitution of their bodies. Sure,
  You ha' not. I'll reserve their waters till
  The morning. Questionless, their urines will
  Inform you better.

Doct.   Ha, ha, ha.

D'Am.   Dost laugh,   95
  Thou villain? Must my wisdom that has been
  The object of men's admiration now

---

74. O] Ooh *Q.*

---

 85. *radical*] pertaining to the moisture or humour which, according to medieval physiology, was present in all living things and was essential to life (*O.E.D.*).
 ability] strength.
 88–90. *Take . . . bodies*] Elixir of gold was believed to have great medicinal powers. There is a fine irony in D'Amville's attempt to use his gold, which he has declared to be the source of all power, in a futile attempt to restore life.
 93. *reserve*] preserve.

    Become the subject of thy laughter?

Rous.   O.   *Dies.*

All. He's dead.

D'Am.   O there expires the date
Of my posterity. Can Nature be   100
So simple or malicious to destroy
The reputation of her proper memory?
She cannot. Sure there is some power above
Her that controls her force.

Doct.   A power above Nature?
Doubt you that, my lord? Consider but   105
Whence man receives his body and his form:
Not from corruption like some worms and flies,
But only from the generation of
A man, for Nature never did bring forth
A man without a man; nor could the first   110
Man, being but the passive subject, not
The active mover, be the maker of
Himself; so of necessity there must
Be a superior power to Nature.

D'Am. Now to myself I am ridiculous.   115
Nature, thou art a traitor to my soul.
Thou hast abus'd my trust. I will complain
To a superior court to right my wrong.
I'll prove thee a forger of false assurances.
In yond' Star Chamber thou shalt answer it.   120
Withdraw the bodies. O the sense of death
Begins to trouble my distracted soul.   *Exeunt.*

---

98. O] Ooh *Q.*   115. Now . . . ridiculous] *Q (corrected); not in Q (un-corrected).*   121-2. Withdraw . . . soul] *Q (corrected); not in Q (uncorrected).*

---

99. *date*] duration.
102. *proper*] own.
119. *assurances*] guarantees of security.
120. *Star Chamber*] the Tudor high court (in which appeals from the Court of Chancery were heard), here used with a play on words. Cf. Introduction, p. xlvi.
121. *sense*] awareness.

[v. ii]

Enter Judges *and* Officers.

1 Judge. Bring forth the malefactors to the bar.

Enter CATAPLASMA, SOQUETTE *and* FRESCO.

Are you the gentlewoman in whose house
The murders were committed ?
Cata.   Yes, my lord.
1 Judge. That worthy attribute of gentry which
    Your habit draws from ignorant respect   5
    Your name deserves not, nor yourself the name
    Of woman, since you are the poison that
    Infects the honour of all womanhood.
Cata. My lord, I am a gentlewoman, yet
    I must confess my poverty compels   10
    My life to a condition lower than
    My birth or breeding.
2 Judge.   Tush, we know your birth.
1 Judge. But under colour to profess the sale
    Of tires and toys for gentlewomen's pride,
    You draw a frequentation of men's wives   15
    To your licentious house, and there abuse
    Their husbands.
Fres.   Good my lord, her rent is great.
    The good gentlewoman has no other thing

---

v. ii. 1.1. FRESCO] *Frisco* Q (*and throughout scene*).

---

v. ii. 1. *bar*] On the Jacobean stage a wooden bar was used to indicate
trial scenes. Cf. G. F. Reynolds, *The Staging of Elizabethan Plays at the
Red Bull Theater 1605–1625* (New York, 1940), pp. 82–3. An illustration of
this stage property may be found in *The Works of Mr. Francis Beaumont
and Mr. John Fletcher* (London, 1711), IV, 1781.
    5. *habit*] clothes.
ignorant respect] the respect given by ignorant people.
    14. *tires*] Cf. IV. i. 67.
toys] trifles.
    15. *frequentation*] habitual attendance (*O.E.D.*).

          To live by but her lodgings; so she's forc'd
          To let her fore-rooms out to others, and   20
          Herself contented to lie backwards.
2 Judge.   So.
1 Judge. Here is no evidence accuses you
          For accessaries to the murder; yet
          Since from the spring of lust which you preserv'd
          And nourish'd ran th' effusion of that blood,   25
          Your punishment shall come as near to death
          As life can bear it. Law cannot inflict
          Too much severity upon the cause
          Of such abhorr'd effects.
2 Judge.   Receive your sentence.
          Your goods, since they were gotten by that means   30
          Which brings diseases, shall be turn'd to th' use
          Of hospitals; you carted through the streets
          According to the common shame of strumpets,
          Your bodies whipp'd till with the loss of blood
          You faint under the hand of punishment.   35
          Then, that the necessary force of want
          May not provoke you to your former life,
          You shall be set to painful labour, whose
          Penurious gains shall only give you food
          To hold up nature, mortify your flesh,   40
          And make you fit for a repentant end.
All. O good my lord!
1 Judge.   No more; away with 'em.
                    Exeunt [CATAPLASMA, SOQUETTE, *and* FRESCO].

                Enter LANGUEBEAU SNUFFE.

42.1. CATAPLASMA . . . FRESCO] *Symonds.*

_____

   21. *lie backwards*] inhabit the back rooms, with a sexual *double entendre.*
Cf. Shakespeare, *Romeo and Juliet*, I. iii. 41–2:
            'Yea,' quoth he, 'dost thou fall upon thy face?
            Thou wilt fall backward when thou hast more wit.'
   32–4. *carted . . . whipp'd*] the ordinary punishment for Jacobean prosti-
tutes.

2 Judge. Now, Monsieur Snuffe, a man of your profession
    Found in a place of such impiety!

Lang. I grant you the place is full of impurity. So much the   45
    more need of instruction and reformation. The purpose
    that carried me thither was with the spirit of conversion to
    purify their uncleanness, and I hope your lordship will
    say the law cannot take hold o' me for that.

1 Judge. No, sir, it cannot; but yet give me leave   50
    To tell you that I hold your wary answer
    Rather premeditated for excuse
    Than spoken out of a religious purpose.
    Where took you your degrees of scholarship?

Lang. I am no scholar, my lord. To speak the sincere truth, I   55
    am Snuffe the tallow-chandler.

2 Judge. How comes your habit to be alter'd thus?

Lang. My Lord Belforest, taking a delight in the cleanness of
    my conversation, withdrew me from that unclean life and
    put me in a garment fit for his society and my present   60
    profession.

1 Judge. His lordship did but paint a rotten post,
    Or cover foulness fairly. Monsieur Snuffe,
    Back to your candle-making. You may give
    The world more light with that than either with   65
    Instruction or th' example of your life.

Lang. Thus the Snuffe is put out.   *Exit.*

Enter D'AMVILLE *distractedly, with the hearses of his*
two sons borne after him.

45. *Lang.] Snuffe. Q (and throughout scene).*

---

    43. *profession*] Cf. above, I. ii. 207.
    62. *paint . . . post*] Collins calls attention to Satire X of Marston's *Scourge*
of Villainy (ed. Bullen), 61–2:
              Juggling Opinion, thou enchanting witch!
              Paint not a rotten post with colours rich.
The allusion, Bullen suggests, is to the posts which stood at the doors of
sheriffs, and which were repainted whenever a new sheriff came into office.
(Cf. Tilley, p. 492: 'As good trust to a rotten post.')
    67. *Thus . . . out*] Cf. above, IV. i. 62.

D'Am. Judgment, judgment!

2 Judge.   Judgment, my lord, in what?

D'Am. Your judgments must resolve me in a case.

    Bring in the bodies. Nay, I will ha 't tried.   70
    This is the case, my lord: my providence,
    Ev'n in a moment, by the only hurt
    Of one, or two, or three at most—and those
    Put quickly out o' pain too, mark me; I
    Had wisely rais'd a competent estate   75
    To my posterity; and is there not
    More wisdom and more charity in that,
    Than for your lordship, or your father, or
    Your grandsire to prolong the torment and
    The rack of rent from age to age upon   80
    Your poor penurious tenants, yet perhaps
    Without a penny profit to your heir?
    Is 't not more wise, more charitable? Speak.

1 Judge. He is distracted.

D'Am.   How? Distracted? Then

    You ha' no judgment. I can give you sense   85
    And solid reason for the very least
    Distinguishable syllable I speak.
    Since my thrift was more charitable, more
    Judicious than your grandsire's, why, I would
    Fain know why your lordship lives to make   90
    A second generation from your father,
    And the whole fry of my posterity
    Extinguish'd in a moment, not a brat
    Left to succeed me—I would fain know that.

---

88. more charitable] *Q (corrected); not in Q (uncorrected), Collins.*

---

69. *resolve*] free from doubt or perplexity. Cf. Shakespeare, *3 Henry VI*,
III. ii. 19–20:

       May it please your highness to resolve me now,
       And what your pleasure is shall satisfy me.

71. *providence*] Cf. I. i. 56, I. i. 112, and I. ii. 51.

80. *rack of rent*] Rack-rent was rent equal to or close to the actual value
of the property being rented. Cf. Clarkson and Warren, p. 96.

2 Judge. Grief for his children's death distempers him.   95
1 Judge. My lord, we will resolve you of your question.
    In the meantime vouchsafe your place with us.
D'Am. I am contented, so you will resolve me.   *Ascends.*

       Enter CHARLEMONT *and* CASTABELLA.

2 Judge. Now, Monsieur Charlemont, you are accus'd
    Of having murder'd one Borachio that   100
    Was servant to my Lord D'Amville. How can
    You clear yourself? Guilty or not guilty?
Char. Guilty of killing him, but not of murder.
    My lords, I have no purpose to desire
    Remission for myself.

       D'AMVILLE *descends to* CHARLEMONT.

D'Am.   Uncivil boy,   105
    Thou want'st humanity to smile at grief.
    Why dost thou cast a cheerful eye upon
    The object of my sorrow, my dead sons?
1 Judge. O good my lord, let charity forbear
    To vex the spirit of a dying man.   110
    A cheerful eye upon the face of death
    Is the true count'nance of a noble mind.
    For honour's sake, my lord, molest it not.
D'Am. Y' are all uncivil. O, is 't not enough
    That he unjustly hath conspir'd with Fate   115
    To cut off my posterity, for him
    To be the heir of my possessions, but
    He must pursue me with his presence, and
    In the ostentation of his joy
    Laugh in my face and glory in my grief?   120
Char. D'Amville, to show thee with what light respect
    I value death and thy insulting pride,
    Thus, like a warlike navy on the sea,
    Bound for the conquest of some wealthy land,

---

121. *respect*] Cf. v. ii. 5.
M

Pass'd through the stormy troubles of this life   125
And now arriv'd upon the armed coast,
In expectation of the victory
Whose honour lies beyond this exigent,
Through mortal danger, with an active spirit,
Thus I aspire to undergo my death.   130

> *Leaps up the scaffold.* CASTABELLA *leaps after him.*

Cast. And thus I second thy brave enterprise.
Be cheerful, Charlemont. Our lives cut off
In our young prime of years are like green herbs
Wherewith we strew the hearses of our friends,
For as their virtue gather'd when th' are green,   135
Before they wither or corrupt, is best,
So we in virtue are the best for death
While yet we have not liv'd to such an age
That the increasing canker of our sins
Hath spread too far upon us.

D'Am.   A boon, my lords;   140
I beg a boon.

1 Judge.   What's that, my lord?

D'Am. His body when 'tis dead
For an anatomy.

2 Judge.   For what, my lord?

D'Am. Your understanding still comes short o' mine.
I would find out by his anatomy   145
What thing there is in Nature more exact
Than in the constitution of myself.
Methinks my parts and my dimensions are
As many, as large, as well compos'd as his,

144. comes] *Collins;* come *Q.*

---

128. *exigent*] extremity.
139. *canker*] a spreading sore or ulcer. The term is used also to apply to
a disease of plants which causes bark and tissues slowly to decay, and to a
species of green caterpillar which destroys the buds and leaves of plants. It
seems clear that the first sense is here intended.
143. *anatomy*] skeleton.
146. *exact*] perfect.

And yet in me the resolution wants   150
To die with that assurance as he does.
The cause of that in his anatomy
I would find out.
1 Judge.   Be patient and you shall.
D'Am. I have bethought me of a better way.
   Nephew, we must confer. Sir, I am grown   155
A wond'rous student now o' late. My wit
Has reach'd beyond the scope of Nature; yet
For all my learning I am still to seek
From whence the peace of conscience should proceed.
Char. The peace of conscience rises in itself.   160
D'Am. Whether it be thy art or nature, I
   Admire thee, Charlemont. Why, thou hast taught
A woman to be valiant. I will beg
Thy life. My lords, I beg my nephew's life.
I'll make thee my physician. Thou shalt read   165
Philosophy to me. I will find out
Th' efficient cause of a contented mind;
But if I cannot profit in 't, then 'tis
No more, being my physician, but infuse
A little poison in a potion when   170
Thou giv'st me physic, unawares to me.
So I shall steal into my grave without
The understanding or the fear of death,
And that's the end I aim at, for the thought
Of death is a most fearful torment; is 't not?   175
2 Judge. Your lordship interrupts the course of law.
1 Judge. Prepare to die.
Char.   My resolution's made.
   But ere I die, before this honour'd bench,
With the free voice of a departing soul,
I here protest this gentlewoman clear   180
Of all offence the law condemns her for.

169. more] *Q;* more good *Collins.*

150. *wants*] is lacking.

Cast. I have accus'd myself. The law wants power
          To clear me. My dear Charlemont, with thee
          I will partake of all thy punishments.
Char. Uncle, for all the wealthy benefits   185
          My death advances you, grant me but this:
          Your mediation for the guiltless life
          Of Castabella, whom your conscience knows
          As justly clear as harmless innocence.
D'Am. Freely. My mediation for her life,   190
          And all my int'rest in the world to boot,
          Let her but in exchange possess me of
          The resolution that she dies withal.
          The price of things is best known in their want.
          Had I her courage, so I value it,   195
          The Indies should not buy 't out o' my hands.
Char. Give me a glass of water.
D'Am.   Me, of wine.
          This argument of death congeals my blood.
          Cold fear, with apprehension of thy end,
          Hath frozen up the rivers of my veins.   200

          [*A* Servant *gives him*] *a glass of wine.*

          I must drink wine to warm me and dissolve
          The obstruction, or an apoplexy will
          Possess me. Why, thou uncharitable knave,
          Dost bring me blood to drink? The very glass
          Looks pale and trembles at it.
Ser.   'Tis your hand, my lord.   205
D'Am. Canst blame me to be fearful, bearing still
          The presence of a murderer about me?
Char. Is this water?
Ser. Water, sir.   [*Gives him*] *a glass of water.*
Char. Come, thou clear emblem of cool temperance,   210

200.1. *A . . . him*] *This ed.*   209. *Gives him*] *This ed.*

198. *argument of*] discourse about.
202. *obstruction*] in medicine, the blocking of a passage in the body.

Be thou my witness that I use no art
To force my courage, nor have need of helps
To raise my spirits, like those weaker men
Who mix their blood with wine, and out of that
Adulterate conjunction do beget   215
A bastard valour. Native courage, thanks.
Thou lead'st me soberly to undertake
This great hard work of magnanimity.

D'Am. Brave Charlemont, at the reflection of
Thy courage my cold fearful blood takes fire,   220
And I begin to emulate thy death.
                         [*Executioner comes forward.*]
Is that thy executioner? My lords,
You wrong the honour of so high a blood
To let him suffer by so base a hand.

Judges. He suffers by the form of law, my lord. 225

D'Am. I will reform it. Down, you shag-hair'd cur.
The instrument that strikes my nephew's blood
Shall be as noble as his blood. I'll be
Thy executioner myself.

1 Judge. Restrain his fury. Good my lord, forbear. 230

D'Am. I'll butcher out the passage of his soul
That dares attempt to interrupt the blow.

2 Judge. My lord, the office will impress a mark
Of scandal and dishonour on your name.

Char. The office fits him; hinder not his hand,   235
But let him crown my resolution with
An unexampled dignity of death.
Strike home. Thus I submit me.   [*Makes*] *ready for execution.*

Cast.   So do I.
In scorn of death thus hand in hand we die.

D'Am. I ha' the trick on 't, nephew. You shall see 240

221.1. Executioner . . . *forward*] *Symonds.*

---

221. *emulate thy death*] i.e., feel as brave as you in facing death.
226. *shag-hair'd*] Cf. II. v. 129.
235. *office*] i.e., of executioner.

How eas'ly I can put you out of pain.—O.

> *As he raises up the axe [he] strikes out his own*
> *brains, [and then] staggers off the scaffold.*

Exec. In lifting up the axe, I think h' has knock'd
    His brains out.

D'Am.   What murderer was he
    That lifted up my hand against my head ?

1 Judge. None but yourself, my lord.

D'Am.   I thought he was   245
    A murderer that did it.

1 Judge.   God forbid.

D'Am. Forbid ? You lie, judge; he commanded it
    To tell thee that man's wisdom is a fool.
    I came to thee for judgment, and thou think'st
    Thyself a wise man. I outreach'd thy wit   250
    And made thy justice murder's instrument
    In Castabella's death and Charlemont's,
    To crown my murder of Montferrers with
    A safe possession of his wealthy state.

Char. I claim the just advantage of his words.   255

2 Judge. Descend the scaffold and attend the rest.

D'Am. There was the strength of natural understanding.
    But Nature is a fool. There is a power
    Above her that hath overthrown the pride
    Of all my projects and posterity,   260
    For whose surviving blood I had erected
    A proud monument and struck 'em dead
    Before me, for whose deaths I call'd to thee
    For judgment. Thou didst want discretion for

---

241. O] Ooh *Q.*   242. h' has] *This ed.;* has *Q.*   245. *1 Judge*] Symonds;
Judge Q.   246. *1 Judge*] *Symonds; Judge Q.*   247. it] it. *Q.*   252.
Charlemont's,] Charlemonts. *Q.*   254. state.] state.— *Q.*   256.
2 Judge] *Symonds; Judge Q.*   262. A proud] *Q (corrected); this proud Q
(uncorrected). Nicoll.*

---

    254. *state*] estate.
    256. *attend*] wait to hear.
    264. *discretion*] the faculty of discernment or decision.

The sentence, but yond' power that struck me knew   265
The judgment I deserv'd, and gave it. O,
The lust of death commits a rape upon me,
As I would ha' done on Castabella.   *Dies.*

1 Judge. Strange is his death and judgment. With the hands
Of joy and justice I thus set you free.   270
The power of that eternal providence
Which overthrew his projects in their pride
Hath made your griefs the instruments to raise
Your blessings to a greater height than ever.

Char. Only to Heav'n I attribute the work,   275
Whose gracious motives made me still forbear
To be mine own revenger. Now I see
That *patience is the honest man's revenge.*

1 Judge. Instead of Charlemont that but e'en now
Stood ready to be dispossess'd of all,   280
I now salute you with more titles, both
Of wealth and dignity, than you were born to.
And you, sweet madam, Lady of Belforest,
You have that title by your father's death.

Cast. With all the titles due to me increase   285
The wealth and honour of my Charlemont,
Lord of Montferrers, Lord D'Amville, Belforest,
And for a close to make up all the rest,

Embrace[*s* CHARLEMONT].

The lord of Castabella. Now at last
Enjoy the full possession of my love,   290
As clear and pure as my first chastity.

Char. The crown of all my blessings! I will tempt
My stars no longer, nor protract my time
Of marriage. When those nuptial rites are done,
I will perform my kinsmen's funerals.   295

---

269. *1 Judge*] *Symonds; Judge Q.*   279. *1 Judge*] *Symonds; Judge Q.*
288.1. *Embraces* CHARLEMONT] *Symonds; —Embrace Q.*

---

276. *still*] always.

1 Judge. The drums and trumpets interchange the sounds
          Of death and triumph for these honour'd lives
          Succeeding their deserved tragedies.
Char. Thus by the work of Heav'n the men that thought
          To follow our dead bodies without tears   300
          Are dead themselves, and now we follow theirs.   *Exeunt.*

FINIS.

296. *1 Judge*] *Symonds; Judge Q.*   trumpets] Trumpets! *Q.*   297.
triumph] Triumph; *Q.*

Lineation

All departures from the quarto are here recorded.

I. ii
121–2. Fie ... flesh] *This ed.;* Fie ... the / Concupiscences ... flesh *Q.*

I. iv
45–56. Can ... Love] *Collins; prose in Q.*
46–7. Of ... prayers] *Collins;* Of ... conuersation, / And ... prayers *Nicoll.*
107–8. Sweet ... cheek] *Q, Nicoll;* Sweet wife / Thy ... cheek *Collins.*
129–31. Why ... not] *Collins; prose in Q, Nicoll.*
131–2. Verily ... member] *This ed.; one line in Q.*
132–4. Verily ... fruit] *Collins; prose in Q, Nicoll.*

II. i
23–7. Set ... memory] *Collins; prose in Q.*
31–8. Ostend ... enemy] *Collins; prose in Q.*
98–100. Charlemont ... overthrow] *Collins; prose in Q.*
115–16. Your ... knave] *This ed.;* Your ... hate ? / Harke ... knaue *Q, Nicoll;* Your ... heart / With ... hate ? / Harke ... knaue *Collins.*
135–6. therefore ... will] *Q, Nicoll;* therefore, / You ... set / Your ... will *Collins.*
137–8. I ... brother] *This ed.; one line in Q.*
146–7. 'Faith ... rest] *Collins; prose in Q, Nicoll.*

II. ii
40–4. Dost ... in't] *Q, Nicoll;* Dost ... knaue. / I ... sawcinesse. / Ha's ... doe: / As ... by / Clap ... with / Thy ... in't *Collins.*
50–1. Yes ... revoking] *Collins; prose in Q, Nicoll.*

II. iii
21–2. And ... Methinks] *This ed.; one line in Q.*
57–9. Or ... Sebastian] *This ed.;* Or ... will.— / A ... man. / I ... *Sebastian. Q.*
59–62. Ho ... man] *Q, Nicoll;* Ho ... set / My ... now, / Like ... mixes / It selfe ... could / Clasp ... man *Collins.*
63–4. O Fresco ... entertain'd] *Collins; one line in Q, Nicoll.*

II. iv

3-4. Passion . . . out] *Collins; prose in Q.*

7-8. 'Fore . . . 'em] *Collins; one line in Q.*

8-10. No . . . come] *Collins; prose in Q.*

11-13. My . . . thee] *Collins; prose in Q.*

18-23. Eternal . . . mischief] *Collins; prose in Q.*

25-38. Dead . . . his] *Collins; prose in Q.*

39-42. Nativity . . . destiny] *Nicoll; prose in Q;* Natiuitie . . . out, / As . . . be / Ashamèd . . . instrument / Of . . . destinie *Collins.*

47-68. Ay . . . worm] *Collins; prose in Q.*

69-72. He . . . tears] *Nicoll; prose in Q;* Hee . . . way. / So . . . poore / Could . . . 'em / Reliefe . . . teares *Collins.*

72-4. Take . . . weakness] *Nicoll; prose in Q, Collins.*

74-80. Why . . . not] *Nicoll (except as below); prose in Q;* Why . . . Nature / Will . . . but / I . . . were / But . . . teares / Has . . . may / Set . . . you / Like . . . not *Collins.*

76-7. O' wisdom . . . now] *This ed.;* O' wisdom . . . these / Wordes . . . now *Nicoll.*

84-5. Here's . . . he] *Collins; prose in Q.*

105-6. Of . . . made] *Nicoll; Of . . . place / But . . . made Q, Collins.*

140-5. What . . . coldness] *Nicoll (except as below); prose in Q;* What! Dost . . . beliefe / 'Tis . . . hot / And . . . vapour / I'the . . . coldnesse *Collins.*

142-3. 'Tis . . . involv'd] *This ed.;* 'Tis . . . An / Exhalation . . . inuolu'd *Nicoll.*

146-51. Congealing . . . hear] *Collins; prose in Q.*

151-62. 'Tis a fearful . . . wink'd] *Nicoll; prose in Q;* 'Tis . . . meethinkes / Graces . . . as / A . . . speakes / Encouragement . . . how / It . . . forbeare / This . . . should / Not . . . home / Which . . . forebeare / This . . . should / Ha' . . . pitfall. / Then . . . winck'd *Collins.*

163-4. At . . . success] *Collins; prose in Q.*

168-77. Our . . . true] *Collins; prose in Q.*

II. v

4-5. No . . . yet] *This ed.; prose in Q.*

II. vi

12-19. I know . . . me] *Collins; prose in Q.*

44-5. You . . . nothing] *Collins; one line in Q.*

63-5. Stand . . . dam] *Collins; prose in Q.*

66-7. Has . . . fall] *Nicoll; prose in Q;* Has . . . is / A spirit. / I . . . fall *Collins.*

III. i

109-10. No . . . have] *Collins; one line in Q.*

III. ii

35-6. You . . . soul] *Collins; prose in Q.*

38-58. What . . . hurts] *Collins; prose in Q.*

III. iii

    54–5. Out . . . you] *This ed.; verse in Q.*

    56–61. No . . . courtesy] *Collins; prose in Q.*

III. iv

    30–1. Much . . . him] *This ed.; one line in Q.*

IV. ii

    50–1. The . . . two] *This ed.; one line in Q.*

IV. iii

    11–22 He . . . king] *Collins; prose in Q.*

    23–4. What . . . perish] *Collins; prose in Q.*

    25–34. What . . . end] *Collins; prose in Q.*

    54. Where . . . night] *Collins; prose in Q, Nicoll.*

    71–7. What . . . skulls] *Collins; prose in Q.*

    78–9. Death's . . . mortality] *Collins; prose in Q, Nicoll.*

    80–5. My . . . entire] *Collins; prose in Q.*

    86–8. Perfection . . . love] *Nicoll; prose in Q; Perfection . . . thee / With . . . give / Thee . . . love Collins.*

    88–90. Love . . . love] *Collins; prose in Q.*

    90–5. 'Tis . . . satisfaction] *Nicoll; prose in Q; 'Tis . . . forc'd / To . . . performe / The . . . author / Of the wrong. / My . . . would / Disburthen . . . satisfaction Collins.*

    96–7. I . . . cannot] *This ed.; one line in Q, Collins; I . . . to / Thee . . . cannot Nicoll.*

    98–106. A man . . . of] *Collins; prose in Q.*

    107–8. The . . . action] *This ed.; prose in Q; The . . . 'em / Altogether . . . action Nicoll, Collins.*

    110–16. All . . . family] *Nicoll; prose in Q; All the purposes / Of . . . ends / Pleasure . . . sweet / Coniunction . . . meete. / Would . . . to / Thy . . . of / His . . . family Collins.*

    117–28. Now . . . else] *Collins; prose in Q.*

    129–30. Shall . . . they] *Nicoll; prose in Q; Shall man / To . . . were / Made . . . they Collins.*

    131–2. O . . . infinite] *Collins; prose in Q; one line in Nicoll.*

    133–9. Omnipotence . . . examples] *Nicoll; prose in Q. Omnipotence . . . doest / No ill? / Or . . . nature / Doe . . . are / You . . . prerogatiue / Of . . . you / Prescribe . . . law / From their examples Collins.*

    140–51. Whom . . . soul] *This ed.; prose in Q; whom . . . command? / I . . . of / The . . . understanding— / Sir . . . in / Your . . . that / My strength / And . . . themselues / With . . . Sir, / I . . . lust, / O . . . flesh / Whose . . . more / Delight . . . breath, / Euaporated . . . soule Collins; Whom . . . you; / But . . . argument / Confounds . . . vnderstanding.— / Sir . . . in / Your . . . strength / And . . . themselues / With . . . neuer / Wrong'd . . . it / On . . . trade / Of . . . delight, / And . . . breath, / Euaporated . . . soule Nicoll.*

    152–3. Infects . . . graves] *Collins; prose in Q.*

    154–9. Kiss . . . do 't] *Collins; prose in Q.*

    160–73. Suppos'd . . . villain] *Collins; prose in Q.*

173–4. Tereus-like . . . to] *Collins; one line in* Q.

175–7. Now . . . Castabella] *Collins; prose in* Q.

178–89. For . . . defence] *Collins; prose in* Q.

191–202. My . . . destiny] *Collins; prose in* Q.

211–21. Why . . . could] *Collins; prose in* Q.

222–7. Leave . . . me] *Nicoll; prose in* Q; Leave . . . done. / (*rest in prose*) *Collins.*

228–31. I' the . . . mountain] *Collins; prose in* Q.

232–43. To . . . phlegmatic] *Nicoll; prose in* Q; To . . . me.— / Montferrers . . . nothing / But . . . coward ? / He . . . of / A . . . now / To . . . water. / The . . . leafe / Would . . . leafe, / Lie . . . commit / A . . . fresh / Warme . . . supply / The . . . owne, / 'Tis . . . flegmaticke *Collins.*

248–51. O . . . air] *Collins; prose in* Q.

251–2. Here . . . body] *Collins; one line in* Q.

252–5. Black . . . was] *Collins; prose in* Q.

256–63. A . . . Committed] *Nicoll; prose in* Q; A . . . in / Any . . . hell. / Why . . . raise / The . . . damnable / As . . . me / To . . . betweene / The . . . was / committed *Collins.*

284–8. Stay . . . ho] Q, *Nicoll;* Stay . . . soundly / So . . . place / So . . . is / Some . . . freedome / Of . . . ho *Collins.*

IV. v

12–13. Mistress . . . you] *This ed.; one line in* Q.

13–15. If . . . abroad] *This ed.; prose in* Q, *Nicoll;* If . . . bed / I . . . liberty / To . . . abroad *Collins.*

16–20. My . . . effect] *Collins; prose in* Q, *Nicoll.*

21–2. Of . . . for 't] *This ed.; prose in* Q, *Nicoll;* Of . . . can / Neither . . . for 't *Collins.*

23–4. But . . . me] *Collins; prose in* Q, *Nicoll.*

25–33. Enjoy . . . me] *Collins; prose in* Q, *Nicoll.*

56–60. Pursue . . . else] *Collins; prose in* Q.

61–86. O . . . sin] *Collins; prose in* Q.

v. i

48–54. What's . . . chamber] *Collins; prose in* Q, *Nicoll.*

62–5. Destruction . . . dream] *Collins; prose in* Q, *Nicoll.*

66–72. Doctor . . . honour] *Collins; prose in* Q.

72–4. If . . . lord] *This ed.; prose in* Q, *Nicoll;* If . . . 'em / Capable . . . Lord *Collins.*

75–90. His . . . bodies] *Collins; prose in* Q.

91–5. You . . . better] *Collins; prose in* Q.

95–8. Dost . . . laughter] *Collins; prose in* Q.

99–104. O . . . force] *Collins; prose in* Q.

104–5. A . . . but] *Nicoll; prose in* Q; A . . . aboue / Nature . . . but *Collins.*

106–22. Whence . . . soul] *Collins; prose in* Q.

v. ii

9–12. My . . . breeding] *Collins; prose in* Q.

17–21. Good . . . backwards] *Collins; prose in* Q.

43–4. Now . . . impiety] *Collins; prose in Q.*

69–83. Your . . . speak] *Collins; prose in Q.*

84–7. How . . . speak] *Collins; prose in Q.*

88–90. Since . . . make] *Nicoll; prose in Q;* Since my thrift / Was . . . why /
I . . . make *Collins.*

91–4. A . . . that] *Collins; prose in Q.*

105–8. Uncivil . . . sons] *Collins; prose in Q.*

114–17. Y' are . . . but] *Collins; prose in Q.*

118–19. He . . . joy] *Nicoll; prose in Q;* He . . . presence. / And . . . joy
Collins.

120. Laugh . . . grief] *Collins; prose in Q.*

140–1. A . . . boon] *Collins; one line in Q, Nicoll.*

142–3. His . . . anatomy] *Collins; one line in Q, Nicoll.*

154–9. I have . . . proceed] *Collins; prose in Q.*

161–8. Whether . . . 'tis] *Collins; prose in Q.*

169–70. No . . . when] *Nicoll; prose in Q;* No . . . Phisitian, / But infuse /
A . . . when *Collins.*

171–5. Thou . . . not] *Collins; prose in Q.*

190–6. Freely . . . hands] *Collins; prose in Q.*

201–5. I . . . it] *Collins; prose in Q.*

206–7. Canst . . . me] *Collins; prose in Q.*

219–24. Brave . . . hand] *Collins; prose in Q.*

226–9. I . . . myself] *Collins; prose in Q.*

240–1. I . . . O] *Collins; prose in Q.*

242–3. In . . . out] *This ed.;* In . . . Axe / I . . . out *Q.*

243–4. What . . . head] *This ed.; prose in Q, Nicoll;* What . . . up / My
. . . head *Collins.*

245–6. I . . . it] *This ed.; one line in Q.*

247–54. Forbid . . . state] *Collins; prose in Q.*

257–60. There . . . posterity] *Collins; prose in Q.*

261–8. For . . . Castabella] *Nicoll; prose in Q;* For . . . bloud / I . . . monument, / And . . . deathes / I . . . want / Descretion . . . power / That . . .
deseru'd, / And . . . Commits / A . . . done / On Castabella *Collins.*

A World of Wonders (1607)

While it is impossible to determine the specific source for the events of II. v, the following passage from *A World of Wonders* (1607) [Sig. K6ʳ] is representative of the many versions in which the anecdote is extant. (See Introduction, pp. xxx–xxxii.)

Moreouer, we reade of sundry women who haue played strange parts with their husbands, through the counsell and aduice of Priests (or Monks) who had some interest in them; but those I will reserue (as reason requires) to furnish out the legend of Ecclesiasticall vertues here next ensuing, (lest it should be said, that for the great respect I haue of womens credit, I should ascribe that vnto them which of right belongs to Church-men.) To prosecute therefore my former discourse (after I shall haue once againe intreated the Reader to par-don me, if I be ouer-tedious in the rehearsall of some of these stories, the better to discouer these damnable deuises, and to breed a lothing and detestation of them, the memory whereof ought otherwise to be buried) I will begin with a fine feate played by a woman of *Florence*, as it is recorded by two Florentines, who haue written of it almost in the same manner. Whilest this Florentine was with her knaue, there came another, to whom (though sore against her will, yet for certaine respects) she gaue entertainment. She then hearing him come vp the staires, desired him that came first, to hide himselfe behind the bed, till she had sent the second away; whom, because she could not dis-misse so soone as she wished, it so fortuned that her husband came whilest both were with her in the house. Then if euer there was poore woman put to her shifts, it was she, seeing she was to answer for them both at once, and to giue a reason of their comming: and as for the second, he could not chuse but be descried, hauing left his horse in the court, thinking her husband had bene gone from home. What doth she then? Marke the wile of a womans wit: she requested him that came the second, to draw his sword, and with an angry frowning countenance to runne downe the staires, and to say as he went, *I vow here before God I will meete with him in some other place*: which when he had done (not answering her husband a word, who asked him what the matter was, but that he wold meet with him some where else, which he bound with a great oath) the good man went vp the staires, and finding his wife at the staires head (pensiue and sore afraid) asked her what the matter was, and why the man whom he met went in such threatning maner? She drawing back towards the chamber, that her knaue behind the bed might heare her, answered, Alas husband I was neuer in such feare in all my life; for here is a yong man within, a stranger whom I neuer saw before, who fled hither to saue himselfe, being pursued by one with a drawne sword. To be short, she handled the matter so cunningly by her prittle prattle (the gallant which lay hid, afterwards affirming that it was so) that whereas she like a villanous queane had done her husband double wrong in one and the same action, yet she made him beleeue that she had done both honestly and wisely, in foreseeing that no such mischiefe should be committed in his house. The good man then hauing inuited the knaue to supper, and furnished him with a good horse, brought him safely to his house to *Florence*. This was the Florentines feate.

Glossarial Index to the Commentary

This index lists words, phrases, and names which have required explanation in the commentary. Words are given in their simple, uninflected forms when inflections are not essential to the usage referred to in the text. When more than one line-reference is given, the word has been used in more than one sense. An asterisk before a word indicates a meaning not entirely covered by the *O.E.D.*